GOODBYE, MONIQUE

Requiem for a Brief Marriage

by

John Nichols

First Edition 2019

ISBN 978-0-940875-12-8

Library of Congress Conrol Number: 2019909769

Printed in the United States

Photographs courtesy of the author

Cover and book design by Kay Matthews

ACEQUIA MADRE P•R•E•S•S
162 El Valle Road
Chamisal, New Mexico

To contact author John Nichols:
P.O. Box 1165
Taos, NM 87571

Also by John Nichols

FICTION

The Sterile Cuckoo
The Wizard of Loneliness
The Milagro Beanfield War
The Magic Journey
A Ghost in the Music
The Nirvana Blues
American Blood
Conjugal Bliss
An Elegy for September
The Voice of the Butterfly
The Empanada Brotherhood
On Top of Spoon Mountain
The Annual Big Arsenic Fishing Contest!

NONFICTION

If Mountains Die (with William Davis)
The Last Beautiful Days of Autumn
On the Mesa
A Fragile Beauty
The Sky's the Limit
Keep it Simple
Dancing on the Stones
An American Child Supreme
My Heart Belongs to Nature

"We had worked together for a year or so, but we had never surfaced and dealt with the emotional conditions of my first marriage. Suddenly, acting on some cue which was not at all obvious to me, Dr. Graham asked, 'What was there about Monique?' I responded, 'She liked the way I rolled cigarettes.' And then, for almost the first time in my adult life, I dissolved in tears."

—David Gelston Nichols, 1972

GOODBYE, MONIQUE

À Monique, que je n'ai jamais connue:
"Au revoir."

PROLOGUE

Monique in Port-Blanc, Brittany, 1935.

11

PROLOGUE

During my childhood Monique was whitewashed
from my awareness by several factors, starting with my
father's grief, and including a jealous stepmother, Esther
"Brownie" Gleason, who had difficulty accepting my
French roots. She and David Nichols suffered a volatile
relationship during their twelve years together. When
they married hastily in 1944 during Pop's Marine Corps
training period two years after Monique's death, both
my new mom *and* my father adopted me in order to prevent my French grandmother, Mamita, from obtaining
legal custody of yours truly. My real birth certificate
was sealed and a false one issued naming Brownie as my
birth mother. With that, Monique was disappeared and
Mamita had no grounds on which to grab me.

Brownie was young, and I was almost five years old
when we met. I had been living for three years with my

old man's sister, Mollie Weld, and her three kids, my
beloved cousins Nan, Tim, and Dalo. We were a happy
trio of playmates. So for me an abrupt change into
the care of a total stranger was a weird surprise, and I
reacted accordingly. I became a difficult child.

Brownie worked hard to win me over. I balked a lot,
but she took loving care of me and I owe her for that.
She read books to me and made sure I was well fed, had
clean clothes, got to school on time, did my homework,
and brushed my teeth before bed. She took us—
me, and her sons Davey and Tim with my father—to
movies, plays, concerts, sporting contests, you name it.
Enthusiastically, she played us records by Erroll Garner,
Charlie Byrd, and Nina Simone. We had a large library
of books to read ourselves, and I doubt I would have
become a writer without Brownie's encouragement to
explore *Wind in the Willows*, L. Frank Baum's *Wizard of
Oz* stories, and Booth Tarkington's *Penrod* adventures.
She also introduced me to the epic Brownies poems
and illustrations by Palmer Cox, marvelous creations
still.

But Monique was my new mom's bugaboo. I know
Pop never got over the loss of his first wife, hence Monique was *always* around. And, of course, she was embodied in my physical self, my looks, and personality.
In response, Brownie insisted emphatically that people
should understand Davey and Tim and I were all three

her blood children. Period. Anything else would be shameful. I converted to this gospel because the harmony in our family depended on accepting her version of my origins. That was the law.

When Dad summoned the courage to leave her in 1956, my stepmother bitterly contested the divorce, demanding custody of my two little brothers *and* me. There followed a woeful battle between them. At age fifteen I had confused loyalties to both sides. In the end, Dad prevailed and I wound up living with him in Bethesda, Maryland, near the Glen Echo Amusement Park. He was still working for the CIA in Washington D.C.

My father scarcely ever mentioned Monique to me, and I honestly didn't know enough about her presence in my former existence to open that can of worms. For sure, I did not understand the depth of Dad's grief and guilt. Yet for me, instinctively, his suppressed emotions formed an impenetrable barrier I dared not breach. Best let those sleeping dogs lie.

Also, while aging I maintained a relationship with Brownie, especially because I loved my little brothers and did not want to lose them. Therefore, I willingly towed the forget-Monique line. I grew up and grew old incarcerated in that silence for almost the rest of my life. This book is an attempt to break the silence before I die.

Both Monique and Dad kept diaries and natural history journals. They maintained a voluminous correspondence with dozens of people, saving all letters they received in return and carbon copies of those they had sent. I have obtained many photographs of David and Monique from their childhoods on. And a crew of my friends and family members on both sides of the ocean have helped, giving me access to these materials when, late in life, I decided I wanted them.

By the time I began this book I had much information but no clear idea how to handle it. Some drafts were a thousand pages long, others six hundred pages, and quite a few in the 320 to 380 range. For years I floundered in TMI. Over a lifetime I knew my father well, we often got together, and we exchanged hundreds of long letters discussing everything under the sun *except* Monique until I started my good-cop/bad-cop grilling of him when it appeared *he* was dying. A book about David Nichols would've been a no brainer, a vivid memoir because I'd spent all of my life with him.

But about Monique I remembered nothing, she was a blank slate to me, gone when I was a two-year-old and then deliberately forgotten by the people who'd known her best. So what kind of *tone* should I use? Was I allowed to *conjecture* on what she might have been thinking privately? Could I put words in her mouth that were not taken directly from her letters and diaries? And given everything I knew about, and had experienced with, Pop, would his reality, his *vitality*, smother Monique in anything I wrote?

Who knows? After producing almost a hundred drafts over a ten year period I concluded that "less is more," and this is the result. Though it took a while, I realized I most wanted a simple portrait of my mom and dad over the four years they shared together, during which I'd been born. It's not the big family saga I first imagined, but it does focus on two of the most important people I have ever loved.

PART ONE

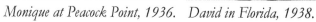

Monique at Peacock Point, 1936.   David in Florida, 1938.

1.

My mom and dad met at the American Museum of Natural History in New York one late October afternoon in 1937. Each held a volunteer desk: Monique in Anthropology (arranged for her by Trubee Davison who was President of the museum) and my old man in Mammalogy (an internship obtained for him by his father through the benevolent auspices of Harold Anthony, curator of the department). Pop's father, my namesake John Treadwell Nichols, was Curator of Recent Fishes at the museum. That is, Grandpa was their top ichthyologist.

My parents fell in love at first sight. She was twenty-two and a half. My future dad had just turned twenty-one. Monique was *enchantée* to *faire* his *connaissance*. While shaking his hand she gave a mischievous little curtsy. Her eyes sparkled and the dimple in her left cheek flew like an arrow into his heart. Instantly, he was a goner.

2.

David Gelston Nichols was well over six feet tall, handsome, charismatic, physically strong, too. Sort of a cross between Gary Cooper and James Stewart, with a *soupçon* of John Wayne thrown in. Also intellectual, although he'd departed the Loomis prep school his junior year and still hadn't applied to college. He was, rather, a budding field zoologist freshly back from a four-month stint outside of Cantwell, Alaska (near Denali), collecting small mammals for the American Museum's Frick Expedition while also playing his guitar and memorizing the collected works of Robert Service, most especially "The Cremation of Sam McGee."

Pop worshipped Grandpa and wanted to be just like him when he grew up. Even before he could read my father had accompanied his father on Christmas Bird Counts at the Floyd estate, Dad's family's summer home. His mentor always smoked a pipe, even in bed, and probably wore the same rumpled Brooks Brothers suit his entire life. It was always covered with ashes, dandruff, and blotches of formaldehyde. Grandpa never listened to the radio or learned to drive, shaved with a straight razor, and only attended movies if they were about wildlife. In 1958 the *New York Times* obituary would describe John T. Nichols as "A tall, lean man, with generally disheveled hair and a wry sense of humor, who was almost typical, in appearance, of the legendary scientist."

Grandpa and my dad roamed all around the Floyd grounds out in the bitty town of Mastic on Long Island fifty-five miles east of New York City. Grammie (Conelia DuBois Floyd Nichols) had inherited that land originally owned by my great (times five) grandfather, William Floyd, who'd signed the Declaration of Independence for New York state. Everybody in our family was so proud of being heirs to "The Signer," you'd have thought we were directly related to Abraham Lincoln.

3.

Grandpa and his youngest son traipsed through the Floyd estate's 613 acres, taking note of black locust and pine trees, red maple and thickets of sassafras and arrowwood. Grandpa identified oven birds and myrtle warblers for his son. At the slightest leafy rustle they pounced on a box turtle or a black snake, and often stopped to luxuriously inhale the scent of foxes, wild grapes, honeysuckle flowers.

They built traps to catch small mammals. Grandpa taught Dad how to prepare museum specimens of those critters when he was only ten. They caught and banded birds together, and glassed plovers running beside the foamy wave lines on nearby Fire Island beaches. Thanks to his dad, my father absorbed the woods, fields, salt meadows, and nearby ocean into his blood, his brain, his personal mythology. Also his ego. By the age of twelve my old man was convinced that one day he would be an ultra brilliant field zoologist, biologist, or ornithologist in line for a Nobel Prize. Not being conceited was never one of his strong points.

4.

Monique was born in Rennes, Brittany, on January 20, 1915, yet she'd been partially raised in Barcelona, Spain, because her dad, Marius Robert, was an engineer who worked there for Gulf Oil until he died of tuberculosis in 1934 at age fifty-one. Monique had lovely blond hair and bright blue eyes that radiated pure light. Occasionally she came on as wiseapple, but there wasn't a mean bone in her body. My future mom was an inventive and peppy girl with lots of imagination, forever smiling, very outgoing, and quite pretty in a healthy way, manifesting her innocence and her good nature, her sense of humor. Although surrounded by professional snobs, she was immune to their pollution. She didn't wear lipstick or fingernail polish, and in younger days her hair was often cut short, like a tomboy's. Her clothes were simple, nothing fancy, but they always looked good on her. Monique had class. As an adult she was five-feet-six-inches tall, and weighed about a hundred and twenty-five pounds.

You would never have guessed that she'd had rheumatic fever as a kid.

Her full name was Monique Annette Andrée Robert. Because she was French, you pronounced her last name "Row-bear." Try to keep that in mind, it's important. I know, I know, she would wind up marrying an American Philistine . . . but she *was* proud of being French.

5.

David and Monique's 1937 romance was an idyll. On autumn weekends they visited Peacock Point and/ or the William Floyd estate, depending. Unintimidated by the imposing grandeur of Peacock Point, Monique expertly maneuvered Dad around the brick Georgian mansion surrounded by Goggie Davison's acres of elaborate flower gardens located on Long Island's north shore, twenty miles east of New York. Goggie was the widow of Harry Davison, who'd died of a brain tumor in 1922 while he was a masterful partner of the financier, J.P. Morgan. But his millions had traveled on. My French family was connected to the Davisons by the marriage of my great-grandfather—a famous writer from Brittany named Anatole Le Braz—to Harry Davison's sister, Mary, whom everyone called Auntie May. She was Anatole's third (and final) wife. Immediately after those elderly lovebirds got hitched, my French relatives had gleefully adopted Peacock Point as their U.S. *pied-à-terre*. Its lavish Big House welcomed them.

6.

Auntie May first brought Monique to visit America in 1931 when my mom was sixteen. All the Davisons, especially Goggie (their powerful matriarch), and Trubee (her eldest son), fell in love with Monique. I remember Goggie in her old age as very plain looking, always decked out in long frumpy dresses and granny shoes, and toppered by an array of oddly flowered hats that rarely left her head, even indoors. Around the estate she drove an elegant black 1922 Detroit electric car, her signature vehicle which never hit the crowded open road. It remained on the paved driveway circling the Tadpole Pond and a few large weeping willow trees that cast afternoon shadows across croquet wickets set up on the closely-cropped greensward.

I recall riding in that car beside Goggie as a six-year-old kid sucking on a lolliop and feeling like the Pasha of Constantinople while we sped along at the vertiginous speed of three miles an hour!

7.

Trubee Davison I scarcely recall at all, yet I owe him everything. He was a man of influence and prestige who flew his own airplane. He also crashed it once into Long Island Sound and suffered crippling back pain for the rest of his life. In 1925 President Coolidge had appointed him to lead a National Crime Commission organized to combat the mayhem caused by Prohibition. A dynamic leader, Trubee was featured on the cover of *Time* magazine. President Harding had made him Assistant Secretary of War for Aviation. A stalwart Republican, Trubee also served in the New York state legislature. And after his wealthy father died, Trubee became a trustee of the American Museum of Natural History in New York, filling a position held by his late dad. A decade later Trubee was elected President of the museum by those trustees, hence he was able to obtain for Monique a sinecure in Anthropology the spring of 1937, which assured that my mom and dad would meet, and, coincidentally, that I would be born and grow up to write this book.

It's an ill wind that blows no good!

8.

I have to believe that Pop's first encounter with the butlers, chauffeurs, maids, and yacht captains at Peacock Point was pretty trippy. I mean, the Big House reeked of Italian marble flooring and had a trophy room full of lion, rhino, and water buffalo heads. In Dad's family people did not flaunt their dollars, they pretended to be reserved and dignified New England Puritans. Yet their wooden colonial Floyd house oozed historical cachet. Dating from about 1720, it had no phone, used kerosene lanterns at night, and, during summer residency, Grammie hired a nearby Poospattuck Indian cook named Abbey. That said, the rickety old house did boast twenty rooms served by five flush toilets. The Nichols' year-round home in Garden City (close to New York), was comfortable, but nothing to brag about.

My humble Dad never called his summer home "the William Floyd estate." Please. He called it "the old family farm." You have to roll your eyes a little over that one.

26

9.

During their weekend courtship days at the Floyd digs, Monique and David canoed from Indian Point over to Fire Island where they tracked shore birds through binoculars and gathered shells on the beach. If Pop and his girl came across skates' eggs on the sand, my father explained them to her. According to David Nichols, what he didn't know about the natural world hadn't been invented yet. Monique nodded sagaciously (and tried not to roll *her* eyes).

The infatuated couple ambled downwind barefoot holding hands while sandpipers ran ahead just out-of-reach of the incoming wave lines. My mom let go of Dad's fingers, lifted her skirt, and scampered into the salty foam, laughing, then ran back, grabbing his hand again. Herring gulls glided low above the breakers. My father found a perfectly round moonstone which he gave to his new girl. Monique kept that pretty stone in her jewelry box for the rest of her life.

10.

They proceeded through forests along the Floyd estate's sandy roads, and, whenever a bird called, Pop identified the call, teaching it to his new flame. If an oven bird or a towhee crossed the road, my father named it in English and Latin, and Monique pronounced the Latin moniker repeatedly. She scribbled every name on a tablet in order to memorize each one. She was smitten. For whatever reason, this man felt to her like the Real Thing.

Monique had never known a "naturalist" before. She had never parlayed with a person who paid so much attention to insects, birds, and owl vomit. He actually picked up deer pellets and *sniffed* them. An entirely new universe was opening up to her. Their future together was going to be so exciting. My father-to-be was bonafide *sui generis*.

However, Monique was no dumbbell. Although my dad came across as handsome and very smart, she realized he was also clumsy, arrogant, insecure, very funny, terrified of girls, socially inept, overconfident, and unctuously self-deprecating.

And she did wish he would *bathe* a little more often.

11.

Monique herself had no formal education, yet she had been all over Europe growing up thanks to her mom, Maggie Robert Le Braz, whom we all called "Mamita," the younger daughter of the Breton writer

Anatole Le Braz's first wife, Augustine Le Güen. (Anatole's second wife, Henrietta Porter, a Baltimore, Maryland harpist, had only lasted three years with the august writer before dropping dead.) An imperious woman who carried a Spanish fan and wore little hats with veils, Mamita was known as "the Elsa Maxwell of Barcelona," and she loved to party down with counts and countesses, bankers and famous cabaret singers, and rich entrepreneurs. Truman Capote would have loved her. Because of her mother's travels, remarkable contacts, and cultural snobbism (added to Auntie May's elegant tutoring when Mamita and her hubby, Marius, were doing time for TB in Swiss sanatoriums, which was often), Monique could speak four languages and read books in six, and she knew everything about ancient and modern art, operas, and films and theater works and European history, plus she could play guitar and sing hundreds of songs in French, English, Spanish, German, and Italian, and she also danced flamenco, typed fifty words a minute, drove a car, and rode horses . . . but she would *never* have bragged about any of this stuff to my dad. Heaven forbid! He was the *brains* in their relationship. The Genius in Waiting. And an obedient woman *always* deferred to her man.

At least while they were courting.

12.

As a young boy David Nichols had roamed the William Floyd acreage carrying a .22 rifle. He told Monique that he was so lonely sometimes he thought he would die. With the rifle he shot squirrels and rabbits that he cooked himself and devoured with ardor. Neither Grammie nor his three older siblings— Floyd, John, and Mollie—liked this cuisine. They thought it weird, aboriginal. Naturally, that was the point. Dad's two elder brothers and sister ignored him, never including him in their social lives and adventures, and his oldest brother, Floyd, beat him up a lot just on "general principles" because Pop usually asked for it as he was such an immodest know-it-all.

Grammie worried that her youngest boy would become a one-trick pony, an illiterate oaf, a moron wearing a loincloth and booties made of marmot skins squatting above some embers gnawing on thawed mammoth bones. To her way of thinking, the wayward lad needed intellectual refinements, social connections, and academic degrees in order to make money. Scarfing small furry mammals was *not* a proper way to achieve these goals.

However, Grandpa was right on board with broiling squirrels because eating the innards of your specimens was part of the Scientific Method, and Grandpa himself—as a respected naturalist and the head of fishes at the American Museum—had often chowed down on willets, stilts, and semipalmated plovers, picking his teeth with their wee little bones.

As for Monique? Impulsively, she threw her arms around Pop's neck in order to kiss him on the cheek, demanding that one day he must cook for her a squirrel. And she promised to eat it. In fact, she couldn't *wait* to eat a squirrel. Lock, stock, and bushy tail. *"Je serai très contente de bouffer avec grand plaisir ton ravissant écureuil!"* Would he serve it in gravy created from a gourmet roux? Then wrap the beast in bacon and stick in some cloves to spice it up?

13.

Pop's mouse traps located across the Floyd estate's meadows and hardwood forests provided much entertainment. At the kitchen table my dad carefully skinned the voles, shrews, and other victims, showing Monique how to prepare museum specimens. Seated beside him she studied her new love's scalping techniques. Mouse guts didn't faze her at all. Soon she could use a Q-tip like a pro to swab the gray matter out of a miniscule skull. Monique was not squeamish. Rather, she was a sponge, retaining reams of information. After a few days with Pop at the Floyd estate she was prepared to skin small mammals and learn stenography in order to aid his work by taking dictation and then typing up his bird and animal data, or copying it perfectly, by hand, into his nature journals. David Nichols could not believe his good fortune. Already, Monique had abandoned her interest in anthropology and was determined to become a naturalist herself, a field zoologist like her man. Love is a magical potion.

My future parents stood beneath oak trees and called in crows. Or rather my father lured in the corvids and Monique mimicked his raspy notes. It didn't take her long to become a proficient squawker. Pop told her the names of specific trees. Monique was particularly impressed by the enormous linden at the west side of the Floyd house—it had been planted over a century ago. And pretty soon she climbed halfway up the tree ahead of my old man calling down to him, "Last one to the top is a rotten egg!"

Many years later Dad told me, "I didn't know then that there was anything wrong with her heart."

14.

Monique and David became engaged on March 23, 1938. I have no record of how they celebrated, or how their respective families acknowledged the event. Mamita, Monique's younger sister Ninon, and her adolescent brother, Nito, were waiting out the Spanish civil war in Paris where they had fled not long after Monique's dad Marius Robert died in 1934. By then the violent conditions in Barcelona had made that city ultra dangerous for the bourgeoisie. And nowadays the Roberts were also apprehensive about the growing probability of World War II and a possible German invasion of France.

My father wrote to Mamita c/o Auntie May's apartment at 9 Avenue de l'Observatoire in Paris. Sadly, Auntie May had died two years previously, breaking Monique's heart. I believe Goggie Davison was now paying the apartment's rent. Announcing his intention to marry her daughter, Pop informed Mamita that no date was set. He and Monique might have to "wait for years." Furthermore, "I have no money or immediate prospects of a permanent position in the field of Natural History." He ended by allowing it was his sincere hope "that the intimacy of Monique and I will extend between our families with pleasure and happiness added on both sides of the ocean."

When Mamita read that letter she must have had an attack of the vapors, a conniption, or, more to the point, she probably shit a brick. *Merde alors!* I picture my hefty French grandmother slumped on a sofa reading and rereading Dad's words while flapping a Spanish fan before her plump flushed cheeks. "No money" and "no immediate prospects?" What else could he have said to plunge the dagger up to the hilt in her ample bosom— "I'm also a homeless leper?"

15.

The newly affianced couple had little time for romance, however, because Monique was booked to go home on a ship by mid-April, 1938. Simultaneous with her departure, Pop headed off on an ill-fated museum collecting expedition to Florida with his pal, Bill Buchanan, and another guy named Ward. They were commanders of a traveling lab trailer invented by the Mammalogy curator, Harold Anthony, who had no idea how to design a traveling mammal lab. Dad would be "catching, skinning, weighing, measuring, labeling, and stuffing small mammals" for the American Museum. The trailer had bunks, a stove, specimen preparation supplies (such as arsenic powder to protect pelts), water, gas, oil, shelves of traps, containers of peanut butter, oatmeal, raisins, and bacon (for bait), and other scientific equipment. It was sort of like a Rube Goldberg contraption built by a complete idiot . . . and a total white elephant. Each time the trailer hit a bump, Campbell soup cans and Spam tins crashed to the floor, coffee pots tipped over, boxes of arsenic powder burst open. Every other day they had to patch a flat tire or repair a broken axle. The bunks were so short and narrow they felt to the boys like cramped coffins for midgets and nobody could sleep. A dogsled pulling a steamer truck full of mothballs through the Everglades would have been more appropriate!

Pop followed the sorry trailer in a 1934 Chevrolet coupe he called the Grease Pig. Who knows how he bought that car? Family dollars, I suppose. Midway through the rolling lab adventure my father judged it "the toughest job I've ever been on from a scientific, emotional, and physical point of view. God has visited most of my vitals with aches, pains, and other distempers."

16.

I've got a photograph of Dad in Florida back then. He is wearing no clothes except for a fedora, a tiny brief-style bathing suit, and white socks and lace-up boots. Standing on a wooden walkway with bay water on either side, he's holding his clothes in his left hand. They droop onto the wooden slats. Head tilted back, Dad is laughing uproariously. His bare torso and skinny arms and legs would be appropriate on a concentration camp internee. All his ribs are exposed. He is practically skeletal and can't weigh much more than a damp feather stuck into a fried popover. He looks like a kwashiorkor victim from Bangladesh. Hence one wonders: *Why is this man laughing?*

17.

On the same April day that Monique kissed my father goodbye and climbed aboard the "M.S. Lafayette" for her return to Europe, she penned him a sweet letter. Here is the abridged version:

"My darling, I miss you terribly, I feel lonelier than I ever have before, we are very lucky to have been able to see each other so much in the past months, and if two people ever had something beautiful to look forward to, we have, Dave, we're just starting, I promise you to take the best of cares of myself, sweet, I'm going to spend these months away from you trying to make myself better in every way so that by the time you are ready for me, I can give you more, Dearest, I'm the luckiest girl on earth, the happiest and the proudest, I still don't know why you picked me out, I long to be with you with all my heart, God bless you, sweetheart, may I kiss you goodnight, your fiancée, Monique."

18.

    Let's face it, though. At this point in his life my dad was a remittance man. He had a desk at the American Museum, but no salary, only the modest expenses due an apprentice, and mere pennies for each specimen he contributed to the museum. His survival depended on an allowance of $38.00 a month from Grammie and Grandpa, occasional checks from Grandmother Nichols (Grandpa's mom), and regular "temporary loans" wheedled from his parents on the grounds that they would be repaid as soon as the museum put him on salary. Though already the black sheep of the family, Pop was the "precocious" black sheep, the scientific genius being groomed to inherit Grandpa's mantle as a gifted and well-known naturalist. Dad's older siblings (Floyd, Mollie, and John) were genteel everyday citizens who lacked their little brother's intellectual skills, colorful guts, and impetuous imagination. In other words, they were sane.

19.

    In May, 1938, the *Journal of Mammalogy* published Pop's notes on the American house mouse, *Mus musculus*. The house mouse was Dad's "totem animal." Fortified by the article, my old man decided to strike while the iron was hot and he contacted Harold Anthony at the American Museum, asking him flat out for a salaried job in Mammalogy. No more unpaid volunteer slavery for him. He was engaged, he had responsibilities, he needed *security*. Then Pop opened his fat mouth and wrote a letter to the museum's president, Monique's friend and ally, Trubee Davison, in which he took the liberty of advising Trubee why his Mammalogy Department needed a uniquely skilled man like David Nichols to put into order, and then study, the museum's collections, which he feared ". . . may end up where the British Museum's rodents are now—in a hodgepodge of disorderly uselessness . . . and in danger of sliding into quiet confusion."

His posting to Trubee ended: "I have been very blunt. I am not a diplomat, but assure you I remain very respectfully yours, David Nichols."

20.

Lots of luck.

Being "very blunt" and "not a diplomat," plus a nickel, might have gotten my father a cup of coffee or a ticket onto the Staten Island Ferry. But it did not secure him a job at the American Museum even though Grandpa was an icon there. The Mammalogy director,

38

Harold Anthony, shot him down like a plastic duck on a carnival treadmill, declaring that museum finances were so bad that, "far from adding new members, the present staff have had to take a cut in salary. The best advice I can give you is to dismiss the American Museum as a salary proposition and if you have an opportunity to get into paying work somewhere else, do so."

And Trubee Davison's goodbye note, though polite, was brutally curt. "We cannot do the job properly without additional funds and I am keenly aware of the fact that this is an awful time to raise money. Best of luck to you."

21.
Damn.

Okay, on to Plan B. Clearly, no future awaited Pop at the American Museum, so he abandoned the traveling mammal lab and aimed the Grease Pig toward California, stopping along the way to collect small rodents in New Orleans, Houston, Las Cruces, Phoenix, Las Vegas, and Reno. The specimens he obtained could always be sold to various museum collections, bolstering his exchequer. In Berkeley he would enroll at the University of California ("if possible") in order to obtain a college education, majoring in Zoology and minoring in Slavic Languages, specifically the Russian idiom. I'm not sure how he got *that* flea in his ear, but often my old man's fey motivations were cloaked by a dense fog of ambiguity. In later years he claimed to have become obsessed with learning Russian because the Soviets were publishing penetrating (and untranslated) articles about *eumetopias*, the endangered California sea lions. Too, the Communists probably knew more about Pop's specialty, *Mus musculus*, than all the rest of the world's mouse specialists combined. Stalin, the rat, promoted his own kind.

22.

Obviously, Dad was in desperate straits as he puttered across America in the Grease Pig headed toward an incoherent future. What he *did* possess during his travels, though, were dozens of enthusiastic letters from his fiancée that arrived daily. Every post office along the way held a batch of amorous tracts for him. Monique was responding to all the loving pages he bombarded her with regularly. Her adoring innocence must have been great balm to my dad's ego.

For example:

1.) "Dave, my dear, you *are* a magician! I can find no other explanation for the fact that every morning, when I wake up, there are from one to three letters from you waiting to be read. Oh, dearest, I love them so!

Thank you for the drawings, sketches and pen and ink reproductions of the animals and things around you. Please don't tire of doing it. They help me imagine your environments, show me what they look like, and, anyway, *I like them.*"

2.) "My little puffin, a kind lady who wanted to be very complimentary and sweet, told me the other day that I was a mixture of Katherine Hepburn and Shirley Temple! It was hard to keep a straight face. I'm sure she goes to the movies too often!"

3.) "My dearest Dave, your letters fill me with so much happiness, joy, contentment, thoughts, comfort, interest, and every one of them brings me closer to you, makes me realize more and more every time that I am not dreaming, that you are there, that we're engaged to be married and to share each other's lives, sorrows and joys, together."

23.

The little puffin arrived in Berkeley at the end of July, 1938, and somehow finagled his way into fall semester at the University of California as a "special student." His address was given as the Museum of Vertebrate Zoology in Berkeley. Then he rented an apartment. The man was unemployed and searching for work; he had two pairs of socks with the toes worn out and no woman to darn them. He was hopeful that Grammie and Grandpa would continue his allowance of $38.00 a month for "two more years." If they cut him off now his name would be "mud," but why think about that? When the time came perhaps manna would fall from heaven. Maybe Grammie, in an irrational moment of magnanimous stupidity, would suddenly sell the Floyd estate on a bizarre whim and give him his cut of the loot!

Meanwhile, Pop really hankered to share his own life with Monique. What was the point of living alone any more? "A lonesome life is hard and very undesirable," he noted. Dad had a tough row to hoe and Monique would "help me to hoe it." She loved and believed in him completely. She was besotted with his intelligence and charisma. His fiancée was becoming a birder in Paris, and already she had proudly skinned, stuffed, and quite competently stitched up *three* whole mice. To boot, she was eager to cook his meals and sew his clothes—what more could a young man want?

Although Pop needed Monique *now*, she began faintly lollygagging. Fewer letters arrived. He experienced uncomfortable premonitions. Then when word from my adoring future mom turned up one day postponing her American trip to get hitched because her sister, Ninon, had been locked in a terrible funk as her pending marriage to an Italian soldier seemed about to self-destruct, my dad got scared.

The coolish tone of Monique's letter was very different from her previous epistles. His fiancée seemed a bit remote, a tad unenthusiastic. The old man felt chilly goosebumps ripple up his arms and across the top of his scalp like hungry little snakes wriggling toward a wounded mouse.

24.

Also, nobody could ignore that the European situation was growing dismal. In Munich, France and England were negotiating the Sudetenland question with Hitler under threat of total war. Already, the Führer had occupied the Sudetenland and Germany was activating a million reserve soldiers. The Luftwaffe had bombed Guernica in Spain. Mussolini was expelling Jews from Italy. Japan had promised it would back the Nazis and the Italians with arms if necessary. And France and Britain had called for partial mobilizations.

Nevertheless, in a cocky, jocular communication to his brother John only a few weeks after his fall classes began, Dad remarked blithely: "As I eat my lonesome meal in the evening, I have a feeling that an emotional bombshell is going to drop on my head from my family, Monique's family, and all the people that consider themselves our family. Let Her Rip! I've made up my mind on a course of action."

25.

Fair enough.

It ripped, and my old man got clobbered.

On September 30, the same day that England and France signed the disastrous Munich appeasement agreement with Hitler and Mussolini that guaranteed the holocaust to follow, Monique broke the bad news to Grammie instead of to my father.

Paris, September 30, 1938

Dear Mrs. Nichols,

I have been going through hell for the last two weeks. My world has fallen to pieces. The dreadfulness of it is that it is Dave's world as well as my own.

Everything that meant life itself to me, Dave, our life together, our hopes and dreams, our future with its joys and struggles, suddenly turned to ashes.

One day I was so wonderfully happy, making plans, working every second of the day to learn things, anything which would be useful or helpful to us both. The next, I woke up so tired and it all seemed so far away, so remote.

Berkeley suddenly loomed up so far away. Four years there seemed so long. The joy of doing things for Dave, of working so that his home would be lovely and lovable, turned into tiresome, tedious little everyday housekeeping jobs and I felt I wouldn't have the courage or rather be capable of doing it.

I was not feeling well and Mother had my uncle, who is a heart specialist, look me over. You know I had a bad heart as a child? I have always been careful of it and so have managed to keep it in good shape. But my uncle repeated once more his recommendations to be careful of it. My Mother told him of what our life would be for the first years at least of our marriage, doing everything ourselves. He said it was absolutely out of the question unless I wanted to be a sick woman on Dave's hands in a little while.

Don't misunderstand me, Mrs. Nichols. I am not trying to give this as an excuse. I won't blame my health. I only blame myself. Nothing you think of me can come near what I think of myself. It's so awful to find out you are no good at all.

Europe too has been going through hell. But now it has peace at last. During these days of dreadful anxiety and deadly calm of despair, I have been so close to mine and to France and the thought of leaving them added to my burden.

I know now that I am not worthy of it, that I am a coward in front of the climb to happiness. I've made a hopeless mess of everything . . .

26.
Pop dropped his classes like a hot rock and left for
the east coast on the 9:00 p.m. train out of Berkeley on
October 6, 1938. From his folks in Garden City and
other relatives he begged, borrowed, or stole all the cash
he could wrangle, then sailed off to reclaim his fiancée
right about the time *Kristallnacht* happened in Berlin,
Nazis on a rampage killing Jews at random, smashing
their store windows, setting fire to the synagogues. So
much for "peace at last" in Europe.
    Debarking at Cherbourg, my father traveled by rail
to Paris. Monique met him at the station planning to
break their engagement the minute she laid eyes on him,
but she waffled. He was six-two, handsome, muscular,
a charming guy with a sense of humor . . . and a silver
tongue. That silver tongue said he was hopelessly in
love with her, he would do anything for her, he needed
her, she was "the most beautiful, alluring, sensitive, and
compassionate woman" he'd ever met, their love would
lift them both to "inconceivable heights of happiness,
adventure, commitment." He worshipped her, he would
take care of her forever, they were made for each other,
he "couldn't live without her." Their home in Berkeley
would be "happy and productive," they would "share
everything together," he was made from birth to be

her man for life, and she was made from birth to be his woman. She was "his angel, his guiding light, his inspiration." Without her he was *nothing*. With her he would "conquer the world, climb to the top of the mountain," and their life would be joyful.

She never had a chance.

27.

A day later Monique acknowledged to Grammie, "I have never felt such a sense of complete relief as when I met him at the station. It was a very moving experience. I wish you could have seen us, standing on the platform in front of each other, with both my hands in his, just looking at each other for a long, long time! I think we bridged the gap right then and there. I have never been so glad to see anybody. It seems funny to look back now and think that, even as the train pulled in, I didn't know whether I wanted to see Dave or whether I dreaded it."

In the next paragraph, grateful for the resurrection of her love, Monique disclosed to Grammie that, "All times of day and night, this one thought comes back, 'I don't deserve it all.' Honestly, I think your son is much too good. He didn't even give me a good spanking for behaving so badly!"

And how did she end that letter? How else but: "I

am happy, happy, HAPPY!"

28.

So instead of breaking the engagement, my mom and dad and Monique's family commenced plans for a wedding set to take place on December 12. If this had been more modern times you would have thought Prince Charles was preparing to marry Diana in Westminster Abbey. Mamita arranged two hundred social obligations for my father to meet all the Robert family and friends. Dinners, luncheons, tea parties, cocktails, soirées, coffee klatches, and spontaneous get-togethers at the 9 Avenue de l'Observatoire apartment where the participants spoke French, Spanish, English, German, Flemish, Italian, Catalan, and Dutch with each other, or at least so it seemed to Pop. A Tower of Babel. The gibberish made him cuckoo. They dined at Maxim's and enjoyed Maurice Chevalier at the Casino-de-Paris, and attended several French movies and American movies with French subtitles, and toured the Louvre. Monique's little brother, Nito, who was thirteen, played a stunning piano concert featuring Mozart, Bach, and Beethoven while Mamita's "Belle Epoque" entourage lolled around guzzling tubs of *Moët et Chandon*. David, and Monique's younger sister, Ninon, engaged in a slew of "discussions and arguments." They did not like each other. Ninon was crabby about breaking up with her Italian boyfriend. *Toujours le cafard.* If she couldn't have her Italian, then Monique had no right to her American. All the same, Ninon *was* beautiful . . . and sexy. Pop couldn't ignore that she had feminine wiles her big sister lacked.

"*Tu m'embête,*" Ninon said. "*Ton bavardage est en train de m'écraser.* I'm unhappy. Leave me alone."

29.

Monique applied for her immigration visa. My father converted to Catholicism. Wedding invitations were sent out. Dad mailed Grammie and Goggie Davison a list of American friends to beckon. He begged somebody from his own family to cross the ocean and stand up for him. Big brother Floyd and sister Mollie agreed to appear if Pop promised to button his fat lip and just be *humble* for once. My dad petitioned home for more money. How come?

"The complications of marriage have entailed lawyer's services, doctors, and the fabrication of new clothes for me," Dad grumbled to Grandpa. "I have been pressed into numerous small and some large expenses which I resent a little bit. I am often very much annoyed by Madame Robert's attitude toward her own family and me in regard to money, and the spending of it. However, don't have the feeling that her mother is a tactless old nut. She's not. She's deeply sympathetic, and cooperative with us, and altogether a dear sweet person."

Oh yeah? Dad *hated* Mamita already. Right from the start he had realized that she despised his tacky American roots, his poverty, his lack of education, his fanatical attachment to grody little mice and chipmunks. Pop believed that all the absurd preparations for the wedding were a grotesque charade. And the totally irresponsible money outflow that Mamita insisted upon was going to bankrupt him. *She had no common sense!*

Still, he must keep his mouth shut. He was not allowed to fly off the handle, read her a riot act, hogtie her with rope from top to bottom, shove her into a tumbrel, and cart her off to the guillotine where she belonged.

30.

Then the Paris town hall made it nearly impossible to obtain a permit for the civil wedding. Monique crawled under the covers for two days because she couldn't stand the melodrama. Mamita repaired to *her* four-poster with catarrh. Ninon had been festering in sick bay with a throat gland infection and a broken heart over her now shattered Italian engagement. Pop took long walks alone around Paris wondering if his "course of action" was more like pissing into a category 5 hurricane.

Next, the French government passed a law decreeing that foreigners could not marry French citizens without a two years' residency in France. My dad needed a *"carte d'identité."* Obviously, he did not possess a French identity card. An underling at the American Consulate suggested that Pop ask a politically influential American, if he knew one, for help. Then French authorities might waive the technicality. Dad cabled Grandpa, pleading for a miracle. Grandpa typed a letter to the American President, Franklin Roosevelt, whom he had bumped into on occasion.

"Monique is quite French," he advised FDR, "but has been in New York a lot visiting the Davisons, connections of her family by marriage. Trubee Davison as you know is now president of our Museum. The wedding seems an appropriate one, the children are much in love and will be bitterly disappointed if it even has to be postponed. We will all be most appreciative of anything that may be done from Headquarters to facilitate it."

"Headquarters" promptly cabled the Frogs, and the Frogs waived the identity card technicality, thus Monique and David were joined in matrimony on December 12, 1938. To compound the miracle, Grandmother Nichols chose that moment to cable that she'd contribute a hundred bucks a month to the young couple for at least the first year of their marriage, maybe longer. Thank you, Jesus! The wedding occurred in a small chapel run by nuns who were friends of the Robert family. A salon attached to the chapel provided dining and the music of a harp, a violin, and an organ. The altar and salon were decorated with heaps of white flowers as if for the funeral of a mafioso don. Monseigneur Chaptal, a vice-cardinal, presided. My dad wore a custom-made cutaway in which he felt like "an embalmed penguin," and my mom's dress was of "stiff taffeta with a very simple bodice." Her heart was bouncing around like a *pelota* in a jai alai *frontón*.

Mamita must have looked on with a gimlet eye, paralyzed with shame that her beautiful and cultured French daughter was really getting hitched to this ignorant, irresponsible, and penniless American *clochard*. Yet she smiled and hugged all the guests, kissing both their cheeks, drank enough champagne to float a battleship, and unctiously toadied up to my father, his sister, and brother as if they were royalty personified.

One thinks of Machiavelli *and* Uriah Heep.

31.

Next day, even before you could blurt "Jack Robinson!," the newlyweds were on the "Champlain" headed for New York. My father couldn't get out of Dodge fast enough. Monique wondered: *What in the name of God just happened to me?* In America, they hung out for one night in Garden City celebrating Christmas with Grammie and Grandpa, then departed on a train for California, putting as much distance as possible between themselves and family, eager to be on their *own*. They'd just been through a six-week-long, highly disorganized, totally intimidating, traumatic (and financially expensive!) emotional kerfuffle that had pretty much disabled them both. Holding hands, they took some very deep breaths. Alone, together, at last. Monique was exhausted and more or less shell shocked. What a year *this* had been! Her heart was acting up with little spasms. Occasionally, she felt terribly apprehensive about what lay in store. Separated from her family, her culture, and from her country preparing for war, she was also exhilarated and madly in love (again) with her new husband (who was unemployed and had no idea how to earn a living, get a college degree, make love with a woman, or take care of a wife). Monique gripped Dad's arm and inclined her head against his shoulder seeking solace and reassurance even as she somehow considered herself the luckiest girl in the world.

For sure, there was no turning back.

PART TWO

Dad seranading Monique, end of 1938.

32.

The first week of January 1939 my future parents set up housekeeping in a modest four-room apartment at 1713 Dwight Way in Berkeley as 22,000 Nazis assembled in New York's Madison Square Garden sang "The Star Spangled Banner" and recited the pledge of allegiance. Across the ocean, Francisco Franco's troops occupied Monique's hometown of Barcelona and the fascist retributions began. Despite those travails, Mamita, Ninon, and Nito looked to Spain from 9 Avenue de l'Observatoire in Paris which was not all that distant from the German border where French and Nazi troops were gathering as war paranoia grew. Soon the Roberts' exile from Spain might end even as France prepared for war with Hitler.

But all Monique wanted right now was to be a Good Wife. Of a sudden her principal job in life was preparing two meals a day, breakfast and dinner, eager to fatten up her husband, although first she must learn how to cook. Fortunately, my dad loved scrambled eggs, bacon, Dinty Moore beef stew, and corned beef hash from a can. After all, this was a man who had already devoured gray squirrels, rabbits, a Florida muskrat, a great horned owl, several bats, and a host of lemmings from Cantwell, Alaska.

"I am no cordon bleu, I must confess," Monique told Grammie, "but nothing I have cooked so far has been un-eatable." On two different occasions Monique also prepared meals for friends of theirs, "And I didn't poison them," Monique chirped. "They are still alive!"

33.

Monique confided to Grammie that she was now "working every second of the day to learn things, anything which would be useful or helpful to us both." She was committed to "the joy of doing things for Dave, of working so that his home would be lovely and lovable."

But most of all she was stuffing him full of food, yet would like to see him grow a little fatter. She said, "I am taking more and more pleasure in cooking as I go along." And then—surprise! Pretty soon Monique's culinary expertise had buffed up her husband. His wife bragged to Grammie, "Your son now weighs 194 pounds in contrast to his weight of 176 pounds in Paris! No more protruding ribs like in 1938 when he was so ill in Florida. He is pretty strong too and takes advantage of it as when he dumped me in the bathtub full of water with my clothes on the other day!"

34.

Adapting to her new role on the fly, Monique scrambled Dad's eggs, made him drink milk at every meal, and poured him four glasses of orange juice a day for the vitamins to combat colds. My father caught colds like other men catch the commuter train every weekday morning at 7:16. She also darned and mended his sweaters and socks, sewed buttons on his shirts and ironed the shirts, and washed his undershorts by hand in the tub. She cleaned his couple of mouse cages, watered and fed the animals, and, during time outs, played their borrowed piano, teaching Dad the chords to "Saint James Infirmary" and "Bury Me Not on the Lone Prairie."

My old man enrolled in a half-dozen classes. Monique studied German at the university (and would shortly be able to translate German articles on mammalogy). Soon they had many friends, youngsters like themselves who gathered for dinners at tiny apartments, drank beer, played anagrams and poker, and ate "black bread with slices of cheese, cold cuts, and anchovies." Everybody smoked cigarettes and laughed a lot. They were all far-sighted zoologists, linguists, mathematicians, biologists, and they were happy. And whenever Monique and David played guitars together their crowd of pals burst into song, making a joyful noise.

35.

I have a snapshot of Pop and Monique just leaving the UC Berkeley campus, Sather Gate behind them as they step onto Telegraph Avenue. My dad, in slacks, coat and tie, and a V-neck sweater, is tipping his gray fedora and carrying a briefcase. Very dapper. Beside him strides pretty Monique, smiling happily, her outfit a dark skirt, a light sweater and colorful shawl; she carries an armload of books. Her hair is long, drawn back, with a white barrette flower on top. They are young and bursting with high energy and promise, a really attractive couple.

"Being married is *thrilling!*" Monique declared. "We are so *grown up!*

36.

My mom quickly took charge of writing their natural history journals. Monique's cursive script was a hundred times more legible than Pop's caveman hieroglyphics. Overnight, she had become an enthusiastic naturalist. Monique listed all their bird and animal observations, including the Latin names as well. She became a stickler for the smallest detail and didn't miss a trick, determined to be a mirror of her husband, just as her husband had hoped to mirror his naturalist dad. "I have a mind like a steel elephant," she bragged to my father. He pretended to shiver in fear *and* exaltation. She gave him a love tap upside the head.

Monique explained to Grammie: "Perhaps you think that Dave is so interested in birds that I, trying to be a good wife, follow him along. Don't you believe it! I get much more excited than he does about them and hardly give him a breathing spell, now and then, between assaults of questions, descriptions, etc. of some bird I happen to have just seen. But, my goodness, it is so much more fun than a movie or many other amusements!"

37.

Pop continued his small mammal studies, setting traps in the Berkeley hills. While he was at morning classes Monique checked the traps, excitedly bringing home their harvest in a cloth collecting bag. They removed seeds from rodent cheek pouches and sprouted them on cheesecloth and wire netting spread across water trays balanced on their window ledges. When the seeds became mature plants that flowered they could easily identify what food the mice had been eating. The most common was *Salsola kali*, the pesky Russian thistle.

Their apartment soon resembled a cross between a botanical garden, a museum workshop, and a library where tornadoes had knocked half the books off the shelves! Piles of unruly school papers lay on the couch, the counters, the dining area table. Monique liked the clutter, which she had never before experienced. It gave her quite a sense of freedom, abandon, *soaring*, to realize that it's okay to live in a mess. *Un méli-mélo.* Her life had grown so *original.*

Nevertheless, she continued to empty wastebaskets, swept the floors, shook out rugs, made the bed, dusted the window sills, and washed innumerable dishes. With a broom she whacked down spider webs from the ceiling corners. Then she polished my father's shoes and brushed clean the lapels of his suit coats. Dad always wore a coat, a vest, and a tie to classes. They didn't have an ice box so Monique maintained careful order between cartons, jars, and cans in the cupboards. Oranges and avocados neatly occupied a wooden bowl on the dining table.

In this manner Monique kept the disorder "down to a dull roar," an expression my father often used. But he never batted an eyelash if the house was topsy-turvy. That's the way he liked it. And pretty soon Monique did too. She stopped arranging his volumes of Linnean philosophy back in the bookcase when he wasn't around. And sometimes she didn't even fluff the pillows after making up their bed.

38.

The young marrieds regularly played chess and in the beginning he slaughtered her. This is not because Monique didn't understand the game; as a child she'd often competed with her dad, Marius, and also with Auntie May. But Monique was hesitant to put the screws on Pop because in those days women weren't supposed to challenge their husbands. However, pretty quickly that reluctance wore off and Monique turned loose her golem. Though Dad had drubbed her repeatedly she kept coming back for more until finally she whupped him—"Checkmate!"—and unleashed a big chortle.

My father jumped up to spank her for being so obstreperous, and he chased her around the apartment trying to grab hold and wrestle her over his knees. Finally, he backed her into the tiny kitchen closet and yanked shut the door behind them. Oops! Pitch darkness, and unfortunately the door couldn't be opened from inside. They were trapped, roaring with laughter, then began to roast uncomfortably in the cramped space. Pop was afraid to smash open the door because the landlord would scream. His apartment was attached to theirs. But knocking on the walls to alert him proved futile. They called for help, to no avail, then kissed, and kissed again. *"Au secours!"* my mom gasped. *"Le diable est en train de me donner les baisers!"* Fortunately, after much banging of pots and pans against the walls, the landlord, Mr. McAllister, tipped to their dilemma, entered the apartment, and liberated them.

The old goat was not at all amused. So what? As soon as his back was turned, Monique and David giggled, embraced, flopped happily onto their bed, and started making out like bandits.

39.

In that bed at night, every night, they read aloud to each other from a biography of Catherine the Great and also from *Philosophie zoologique*. Really? From *Philosophie zoologique*? By Lamarck? Absolutely. And in *French*? True story. Dad wanted to learn the science *and* the language, and Monique never avoided a challenge. You might not think she had the steel to engage with such obtuse erudition, yet she *embodied* the steel. She never pontificated about her grasp of that knowledge, however. In deference to her husband's remarkable brain power, she kept a low profile and tried not to let her mischievous ironic side get the best of her.

A girl can't be too careful.

40.

A friend gave them a Cassin's finch for a pet and Pop dedicated hours to drawing it while the teakettle steamed and Monique darned his socks and old sweaters or practiced her German by reading a bilingual edition of Goethe's *Faust*. Dad named the finch *Ptitsa*, the Russian word for bird. It sang lyrical tunes from the wooden perch in its cage. My father chatted with the finch in Russian while he sketched. I repeat, he was learning Russian in order to read many Soviet zoological texts that had not been translated into English. Sun shone through the window onto Monique's geraniums arranged along the sill. She drowsed with a smile on her face as the finch chirped and her husband labored away. Always, because of her heart, my mom took an afternoon nap, and sometimes Pop quit his studying and lay down with her, encircling her in his arms.

He talked to her even when she was sleeping. My father had been so lonely all his childhood, all his young adulthood. Now he murmured quietly about leaving prep school at eighteen and traipsing around Florida on his own, trapping small mammals for the American Museum. He followed seagull tracks along pristine white beaches and picked up shells, and maneuvered a rowboat through the maze-like waterways of mangrove swamps. One day a flock of over a thousand white ibises flew past him. "A large alligator gave me the eye." Bright green chameleons were abundant on Pumpkin Key. After two months the museum moved him west to Sutcliffe, Nevada, near Pyramid Lake where he ran trap lines from horseback every day across the desert under a blistering sun that almost killed him with migraine headaches. He shot jack rabbits and antelope ground squirrels for lunch, but kangaroo rat specimens were harder to catch than smallpox, yellow fever, or "a pretty girl who would kiss me."

When eventually he stopped talking Monique opened her eyes and murmured, "'Give me a kiss, and to that kiss a score; then to that twenty, add a hundred more.'" It's a dash of Robert Herrick that Auntie May had her memorize in Paris when she was twelve. After Pop kissed her she closed her eyes, instantly asleep again.

41.

The Grease Pig carried them through a snowstorm over Donner Pass to Tonopah, Reno, and to my father's old stomping grounds of Sutcliffe, Nevada, where during the summer and fall of 1935 he'd almost killed himself harvesting small fry for the museum. An aged hitch-hiker with a violin played the French national anthem, "The Marseillaise," for Monique, who lustily sang along at fifty miles an hour. They placed mouse traps among rock piles and sage bushes just as my father had set them five years earlier, and in the same locations. Brown pelicans on Pyramid Lake posed for their camera; the background jagged mountains were dusted white. If a body wasn't too mangled they picked up roadkill for my dad to skin, pin, and annotate: a ground squirrel, a horned lark, a cinnamon teal.

I have a picture of Monique seated on the running board of the Grease Pig surrounded by the Nevada landscape. In another photo she is squatting by a bush near the roadway, probably checking for a specimen. My favorite image was taken from far away by somebody else. My parents are seen in silhouette, standing between a few dark pine trees. Dad is reading from a guidebook to Monique and she listens attentively. You can tell they are intimately connected. On the back Monique wrote with a sly little smirk: *A charming couple. Background: Lake Tahoe. 6-4-1939.*

42.

They took turns piloting the Grease Pig: fifty miles for Monique, fifty miles for David. When he was behind the wheel, Monique rolled him a cigarette. If she was at the controls, he rolled a weed for her. Sometimes, for miles, they couldn't stop singing together. French folk songs, American folk songs. They blew smoke rings, in unison, at the windshield, competing for who could produce the most and the best.

While passing through the Mojave Desert, Monique kept a record of the birds: mourning doves lined along telephone wires; two hundred geese circling above a vast alfalfa field. One April evening, near Lake Tahoe, they enjoyed a romantic dinner at the Hawthorne Tavern served by Italian waiters wearing immaculate white aprons. After dinner they waltzed to a drum and piano orchestra, whirling around lighthearted and happy. You'd be surprised at the gracefulness of my father. Other diners observed them with envy. Monique loved to dance and floated expertly in his arms. He would always be her Prince Charming.

"We camped out on the desert for the night," she noted in their natural history journal. "Set traps around the camp. Very cold night. Starlit. Moon came up about 10:00 p.m."

They must have whispered "*Bonsoir, dors bien*," and slept like puppies until their eyes popped open to birds trilling at dawn. Had their traps caught anything? They couldn't wait to see. At every daybreak they awoke as eager as children on Christmas morning, exchanged kisses, and then raced to make coffee, scramble eggs, and get on with the sure to be glorious day.

43.

A jaunt to Los Angeles was made so that my father could inspect the *Mus musculus* collection at the L.A. museum: he was writing another article about the American house mouse for the *Journal of Mammalogy*. It would be published on August 14, 1939. On that trip he also hoped to observe black-necked stilts on Anaheim Bay. South of Big Sur, Pop and Monique admired threatened sea lions sunning on the boulders, white froth splashing around them. They camped at Redondo Beach snuggled tightly against each other in a canvas pup tent. It was cold. "*Zut, alors!*" They slept entwined for warmth until frogs awakened them shortly after dawn and a burrowing owl walked into their camp, bold as you please. Lighting a fire, they boiled some cowboy coffee while gulls screeched nearby, gearing up for the day.

At the Natural History Museum they studied the *Mus* collection, taking copious notes. My dad pointed out the pelt variations, length of tails, color discrepancies. Monique nodded; and then she nodded some more, seriously. She wasn't placating Pop but rather sucking it all in. On her pad she scribbled notes. Whatever *he* knew *she* was going to learn. That you could count on as sure as death and taxes and the bright smile on

Monique's face and in her soul.

44.

Every Saturday or Sunday she typed up a list of all the birds they'd seen that week and forwarded the list to Grandpa. Pop had convinced her to copy, in their entirety, his Nevada, Alaska, and Florida field books, which he'd borrowed back from the American Museum of Natural History. He also convinced her to copy his voluminous specimen files that likewise had been loaned by the museum. Dutifully, Monique became like a rabbinical scholar transcribing Dad's Torah by hand. If he'd asked her to she would have penned for him two, three, four Torahs, and then cooked him corned beef hash or a baked potato and gravy for supper. Then they would have gotten into bed and read *Philosophie zoologique* for a spell, and after that they'd have embraced each other passionately while Monique taught him the language of love in French.

Simultaneously, my mother worked up for him a bibliography of everything she could find written about his specialty, the American house mouse. *Mus musculus.* She devoted hours, entire afternoons, whole days to the Museum of Vertebrate Zoology's library searching for articles about these humble yet prolific little vermin. You gave that girl a task and it was like money in the bank. She had become my dad's "right-hand man," his "girl Friday," an indispensable member of their team, helping him achieve the progress he wanted to achieve. She loved doing the research and handing it over to her partner for life.

My father once told me that he remembered holding Monique in his arms and repeating "I love you," in French—"*Je t'aime*,"—a hundred times. *She* did the counting out loud to make sure he got the number correct.

45.

Although Monique and David had no wish to read the newspapers or listen to Dad's shortwave radio, at last they could not help themselves. Italy had invaded Albania in April. Nazi troops occupied all of the Czechoslovak republic with astonishing ease. The Spanish civil war ended at the finish of March when Franco seized control of Madrid without firing a shot. That could certainly affect the future plans of Mamita, Ninon, and Nito if France wound up at war with Italy and Germany, who had just signed a ten-year "Pact of Steel" which bound them economically, militarily, and politically to reinvent Europe and create a "just and lasting peace." Monique's family might be forced to seek refuge back in Spain.

Too, almost a thousand Jewish refugees on the liner St. Louis had been denied admission to Cuba, to the United States, to everywhere. Hitler now threatened war with Poland over the free city of Danzig, which he wished to incorporate into the Third Reich. France and Britain promised to retaliate if he attacked Poland. When Stalin and Hitler signed the Molotov-Ribbentrop Non-Aggression Pact on August 23, 1939, thousands of school children were removed from London to the safety of the countryside. And French children were evacuated from Paris.

Hitler invaded Poland on September 1. The Soviet Union attacked Poland from the east. The two aggressors had agreed to divide the country between them. The United States declared its neutrality. Between a list of forty-eight species of birds seen on a late August trip to Pyramid Lake, and thirty-four species of birds observed around Berkeley on October 7, Monique made this entry in their natural history journal:

"*September 3, 1939, Sunday: England declares war on Germany!*"

46.

Dad contracted another of his terrible colds. He was constantly afflicted with colds. For ten days Monique rubbed his chest and back with ointments every six hours. Then abruptly she herself developed itchy "ringworm-type" spots all over her body. Where did *they* come from?

Mamita wrote calmly from France, which had also declared war on Germany. Nito had passed his baccalaureate at fifteen, a brilliant kid. The family was getting visas for Spain and would return there if the Spanish dictator, Francisco Franco, remained neutral in the war. Mamita withdrew money from the bank and hired a driver to help them travel to Spain in an emergency. She managed to rescue her former cook, Elvira, from a French refugee camp to which Elvira had fled after General Franco captured Barcelona. Mamita sent the cook back to San Cugat, near Barcelona, where—a miracle!—the Robert house was in tact. It hadn't been plundered during the civil war. Elvira's instructions were to get things ready for Mamita, Ninon, and Nito.

Chop chop.

A week later those three returned to Spain, fleeing the disaster about to envelop France. Still, Barcelona was reeling, foodstuffs and gasoline and other amenities were rationed and scarce. Mamita had trouble accessing her European funds from Spain. It was not clear if Franco would declare neutrality and avoid joining the Axis. After all, Italy and Germany had helped his Spanish rebellion triumph: he owed them.

However, Barcelona was chastened and relatively quiet, safe again for the bourgeoisie. All the anarchists were killed or driven into exile.

The churches opened once more; nuns were protected; priests crawled out of the sewers, redonned their cassocks, and began swinging their smoking censers again. If anyone protested against Franco too loudly, or in the rebellious Catalan language, they were shot.

47.

My mother and dad motored north on Thanksgiving weekend, 1939. The Grease Pig went through redwood forests and pine hills to Mendocino where my folks saw their first ever Heerman's gull, a thrill for both of them. They traveled along the wild, picturesque coast past Fort Bragg and Westport. Varied thrushes were abundant. Dad braked to photograph a thrush with its beak stuck in an acorn. The bird was captured and he cut off the acorn to free the thrush. Monique would develop that picture in their kitchen, make a print, and affix the print to a page in one of their photo albums where it has remained, so far, for the last seventy-five years.

A heavy rain fell as David and Monique traversed redwood groves on small winding roads. The country was so beautiful, and yet morose. They paid for a motel room in Scotia, a lumbering town, where the deluge tapered off. All tuckered out, Monique slept dead to the world. When she awakened they avoided talking about the war. Or, anyway, they tried not to mention the war although it was firmly with them, intimately present in everything they didn't say about it. Monique was worried about her mother and siblings, her uncles and aunts and many cousins in France and all sorts of friends across Europe. She cuddled against her husband for warmth, for reassurance, pretending to sleep again. She felt woozy. My dad held her until she conked out. Later, Monique swung out of bed and vomited into the toilet.

Up in Eureka and Arcata they halted often to look at birds and identify trees. My father was delving more deeply into botany. He photographed tall pines while Monique stood beside them giving a sense of scale. Pop's photo journal of evergreen trees would augment work for his taxonomic botany course. Under one picture he wrote: *Note Mrs. D.G. Nichols standing in the middle fore-ground.*

Monique felt strange. She almost collapsed.

The fact is she was pregnant.

Oh, shit.

48.

The first week of January, 1940, Monique was hit hard by morning sickness. She fainted at a Berkeley restaurant, vomited often at home, then caught a nasty cold. Lying in bed for days in a stupor, she tried to write a few thank-you notes for Christmas gifts and listened to classical music on her new little radio sent by Grammie and Dad's sister, Aunt Mollie Weld. One day she opened a letter from her Parisian uncle, Edouard Donzelot, outlining her history of heart trouble since her childhood bout with rheumatic fever. Monique was grateful to have it all spelled out in an official text that she could now show to the American medical world. And to her husband.

She immediately arranged an appointment with a new Berkeley doctor, Rodney Hadden. It turns out Hadden was a great guy, he had a fun-loving sense of humor, and, most importantly, he *listened*.

Monique said: "The thing that pleases me most is that he is taking my heart thing seriously. He said he wanted me to realize that I had a small handicap there (as if I didn't know it!) and that it was very important that I take precautions now, in order to be a good and healthy Mother in the future. And so I turn into a very lazy and leisurely lady!"

49.

But during most of January my mother was bedridden, sick as a dog, with cold sweats, hot sweats, nausea, convulsions, vertigo. Dad carried out all the cooking chores, bringing meals to her bed that included "a delicious tender young roast chicken." Monique took one glimpse at her portion of the steaming bird and upchucked all over it. "*Va-t'en, cochon!*" My dad was humiliated. His perfect wife had turned into a raging guttersnipe. About all she wanted to eat now were boiled potatoes. No salt. No butter. No nothing. Just plain boiled potatoes. "And not too mushy, either." Yet mostly she vomited into a bucket beside the bed. It was even difficult to hold down a glass of water. She slept late each morning, napped every afternoon, and hit the pillow right after dinner, sleeping ten or twelve hours a night. When my dad gently petitioned Monique for a sexual interlude, she opened one jaundiced eye and stared at him in horror.

50.

Pop was cramming nonstop for his classes and juggling too many extracurricular balls at once. Preparing nervously for the arrival of his baby, he got himself elected president of the Slavic Club and volunteered to be an officer in the Cooper Club, a birding operation. Then he organized a group called The Grinnell Naturalists Society, an instant success that experienced ballooning membership which necessitated a meeting over which he must preside, as the de facto president, about once every two days! Obviously, he was careening off the rails. Next, he commenced a house mouse breeding project which had nothing to do with school work. His principal cohorts in the effort were two good pals, Frank Watson and Bob Storer. The Three House Mousketeers. My father snagged some wild mice with have-a-heart traps, interbred them with more docile lab animals, rented a room for the operation, built cages, and encouraged the rodents to be fruitful and multiply. He, Frank, and Bob were intense ornithologists as well. They participated in Christmas Bird Counts and helped keep track of gulls, ducks, and herons at Berkeley's Aquatic Park.

Daily, somebody had to clean the mouse cages, feed the animals, note their measurements, behavior patterns, feces production, food consumption, and fornication success ratios. At times the men were too busy to handle these obligations, so Monique was often Shanghaied by Dad to do the mouse chores. She glared at him, but climbed out of bed and chatted up the rodents in French while filling their drinking bottles with fresh water or scraping their droppings into test tubes, then she returned home, puked, and crawled back into the sack.

The truth is, though, that Monique was honored to be included in the mouse project. She was competent, articulate, insightful, and professional. Those bumbling zoologists *needed* her.

51.

My mother, Frank Watson, and Bob Storer became best friends. Her morning sickness quickly diminished, and Monique embraced the house mouse follies. In return, the guys were properly impressed with her fearless expertise around their squeaky minions. It didn't bother Monique at all to handle them, feed them, measure them, scrub their cages, or hold them up by their tails and kiss their tummies while their tiny feet scriggled against her cheeks. She also helped to keep careful records in the mouse notebooks. "I am a *scientist*," Monique declared, her impish tongue in cheek. "And data is like a *god* to me."

Bob and Frank were astonished by her reliability and expertise. They told my dad he had married a "live one." His reply? "Don't I know it!"

Monique and David, Berkeley, 1939.

52.

A downside to the mouse lab is that Frank Watson occasionally got on my father's nerves. "He is prone to order us around in our house, criticize most of my methods of work, jump to conclusions himself (conclusions which are happily usually correct), and interrogate in a nasty tone of voice almost everything that we state as true or of interest. Last night he almost got himself into a fight by taking me to task for doing the same thing to him by way of retaliation. Assuming that he has an extreme inferiority complex, that he is very brilliant, knowing that he is lonesome, and feeling that I have a good deal to be thankful for in this world, I took great pains to apologize for my indiscretion and have adopted a policy of being very pleasant and polite even though at times I'd like to cut him down with a right to the jaw (which I could probably well accomplish)."

Thankfully, nobody decked anyone. My dad and Frank Watson remained friends and continued to pal around with their other distinguished ornithologist cohort, Bob Storer. They were having too much fun together to become enemies. And anyway, Monique warned Pop, Frank, and Bob that these were precious days and should not be messed with because they were also, no doubt, ephemeral.

"Gather ye house mice while ye may," she cautioned.

53.

The war struck home for real in late April, 1940, when my folks learned that Monique's favorite first cousin Mayette Bouchage's husband, a French soldier named Jean Meyneng, had been killed on the Maginot Line. Mayette was the eldest daughter of Mamita's older sister, Reine-Anne. She and Jean had been childhood sweethearts in Port-Blanc, Brittany. They got married on January 24, 1940, at the Notre Dame chapel of that beguiling seacoast village. Jean was nineteen, Mayette twenty. After consummating their marriage at a romantic Breton hotel, Jean returned to the eastern front where the Germans killed him on April 4. Buried at the front, he was awarded the *Croix de Guerre* and the Legion of Honor. At the Port-Blanc chapel a mass was said for Jean only twelve weeks after he had been married there. A French flag stood by the altar; his decorations lay on a cushion.

A week after Jean Meyneng's memorial service, Monique received a letter from Mayette, mailed two months earlier, which contained a photograph of Mayette and Jean leaving the Notre Dame chapel after their late January wedding.

They were beaming like excited rural children about to enter a traveling circus tent.

54.

Mail from Mamita, Ninon, and Nito arrived from Barcelona weeks, or even months after the fact. My mom had trained herself, at least on the surface, to accept the situation. Her family appeared stable although basic foodstuffs were difficult to procure in Spain. Nito was going to pass two baccalaureates, yet his studies were too easy for such a gifted boy. Civil war had left Barcelona's educational system a shambles and Franco's fascist government on edge. Paranoia infected every level of society. Roundups and executions of Republican sympathizers were going on. Nobody was truly safe.

Europe itself was a graveyard. So, too, Scandinavia. Hitler entered Denmark and bombed Norway in air blitzkrieg attacks. Finland surrendered to Russia after three months of bitter fighting. Allies bombed the Krupp arms factories in Germany, which had invaded Belgium and the Netherlands. Nazi air attacks demolished Rotterdam. Then Brussels fell and the Allies were trapped at Dunkirk, where the great evacuations began. During them over 30,000 men were killed, wounded, or captured. Norway and Denmark surrendered. After a fashion, in a hopeless contest, Holland and Belgium fought on.

55.

My father purchased a bicycle to cut down on gas.

However, instead of simplifying life in order to prepare for Monique's baby, Pop now organized yet another project the spring of 1940, a big one not connected to his schoolwork. He was obviously in some exaggerated form of denial. Early every morning he and Monique drove down to Berkeley's Aquatic Park and observed the bird life for about an hour, making careful notes as they traipsed alongside the narrow, milelong lagoon while mist dispersed above the water. Their intention was to keep a daily record of the avian visitations for a year in order to understand how the park was used, and when and by what birds, thereby establishing the migratory patterns of various species and better comprehending the life cycle of the Aquatic Park itself, which had been constructed between 1935 and 1937 by the Works Progress Administration.

David and Monique tried very hard not to miss a day, traveling together to the park when possible, or, if my dad was sick with a cold, Monique made the trip and took the roll. If Monique was laid up, Pop went alone. Quite often Frank Watson tagged along or covered for my folks. Occasionally, Bob Storer did also. When Monique was by herself she walked along the park's eastern shoreline with her binoculars, a field guide, and a steno pad, then laboriously added her data to their natural history notebook.

This was by far the most important and long-lasting scientific project that my folks carried out as husband and wife together. When Monique copied the bird names into their journals she rarely made a mistake. Her handwriting was very neat. She had a passion for the work, penning the date, the time, the weather, the observers present, and the list of birds seen that morning. Their names were rendered in Latin. My father believed that one day their observations might be useful for an article urging increased protection of the park as a wildlife refuge and as a valuable urban recreation area. Secretly, Monique decided that *she* would write the article. FRENCH ORNITHOLOGIST TELLS ALL! But she never disclosed this ambition to her husband. That would have been impertinent.

56.

My mom had an electrocardiogram at Alta Bates Hospital in Berkeley. Dr. Hadden said it showed nothing unusual. Monique remained reluctant to announce her pregnancy even though the baby had definitely begun to show. "I feel better and better all the time," she boasted. "In fact I have never felt as well and content and happy. I feel as if I were sitting on a hill beaming with benevolence at the whole world!"

Monique gained back the weight lost to morning sickness and now tipped the scales at 135 pounds.

Grammie heard from her that the baby, "Makes me feel all warm and comfy. Not only can I feel it move but I can actually see the little jerks, if you will excuse this intimate detail!"

57.

On another day Grammie adjusted her spectacles to read a note from her youngest son. "Monique is getting sweeter and sweeter all the time. When conditions prompt her to be finicky, jumpy, and scoldy she always catches herself and apologizes and smiles and says nice things about my nasty scraggly plants and apparatus all over the house, thus tearing my heart out and leading me to be sweet and generally causing us to get more and more in love."

Further on he emphasized that, "Monique does a tremendous amount of work for me. It is inspiring. She does catalog cards, bird lists, sticking of photos [in albums], and typing of letters. Yesterday I pencilled out six letters which have been waiting an answer for some time and she typed them while I was washing mouse cages. I quite literally do not have time to file the letters that I write and receive some times, then they are all dumped in a box and Monique does it while I am off tending to something else. When I come in from watching birds at the Aquatic Park I am all wet from perspiration; my clothes are changed; she has a glass of orange juice ready for me. It seems that whatever I do she is always there to back me up and make it complete and well done."

58.

My mother was now making copies, by hand, of all Dad's specimen card files lent by the American Museum, an arduous task. On a weekly basis she also typed up their local bird observations, now concentrated on the Aquatic Park, dispatching them to Grandpa. And at the end of every month she drew a graph of the daily species tally for that month, forwarding it to Grandpa, who always wrote back a grateful note, sometimes even in high school French—"*Je vous remercie beaucoup pour les listes des oiseaux que vous m'avez envoyé*"—and he always signed his notes with a "Yours truly, Dad." That may sound a bit formal, but from John Treadwell Nichols, believe me, a "Yours truly" was like a heartfelt "I love you."

59.

As for her pregnancy that late April and early May, Monique had segued into topnotch condition. "I can feel it more strongly every day but am still rather amazed to find no discomfort connected with it at all."

I can picture my parents in bed, Dad with his palm placed against Monique's belly waiting to feel me move. I must have been asleep because it is quiet in there. So he says with alarm, "What's the matter? What's wrong? Why isn't it moving?" Monique replies, "It's just asleep. *Ne t'inquiète pas.* Don't worry your pretty little head." She loved that expression—"Your pretty little head." "How do you know it's asleep?" he asks. "Because I can feel it snoring. Now go to sleep yourself and stop being a worrywart." That was another of her favorite English words—"worrywart." It made her laugh.

Monique drifts right off to sleep. But Dad lies there wide awake staring up at the ceiling. Insomnia is a rare new experience for him, and it's growing. How could he ever take care of a baby? And Holland and Belgium had just surrendered. Then would France be the next to fall?

60.

Two curt sentences at the head of Monique's Aquatic Park bird observations for June 14, 1940, said: *Paris capitulates. German troops occupy it!*

That's all.

She was devastated by the French defeat. Nevertheless: "We only listen to the news on the radio occasionally and try to lead as good and productive a life as we can. I must admit I shed a few emotional tears this morning thinking of Germans in Paris but then I thought what a wonderful thing it is to think that the beautiful city is spared destruction and I am grateful."

61.

In late June Pop left on a weekend field trip with his botany class to inspect trees, herbs, vines, and fungi. And Monique, now over eight months pregnant, diligently kept the home fires burning. On each day that my father was absent Monique boarded a bus to the Aquatic Park and carried out their daily bird observations, walking a ways, then resting on a bench peering through binoculars and meticulously writing down her sightings, then walking again, slowly, completing the circuit. She was huge and occasionally distracted when I kicked the inside wall of her stomach. Monique resisted the temptation to slap me. Instead, she whispered soothingly to me in French, and then sang a lullaby called "*Fais Dodo*" to calm me down. It worked. She settled on a bench to rest and immediately fell asleep herself, oblivious to my acrobatics.

PART THREE

Mom and Pop with Johnny, Berkely, winter 1940.

62.

NAME: John Treadwell Nichols 2nd
DATE: July 23rd
LOCALITY: 1713 Dwight Way, Berkeley, Cal.
SEX: Male
TOTAL LENGTH: 20 in.
WEIGHT: 7 lbs 5 oz.
LOCAL HABITAT: Alta Bates Hospital
COLLECTORS: Monique and David Nichols
FIELD NO. 1.

That is the birth announcement my parents created. Monique and I remained in the hospital for two weeks. She breast fed me, but did nothing else. My arrival had knocked her for a loop. Grammie came out west to "help" with the birthing process and couldn't keep her mouth shut about how to handle this, how to handle that, how to hold the baby, how to wrap it correctly in a blanket. Our doctor, Rodney Hadden, tried to assure her politely that he knew what he was doing. Grammie fled in a hurry when Pop urged her, not all that tactfully, to stop meddling in his life and take a powder back east to where she belonged. My dad's first written comments about me were, "He does not look beautiful and he did not come easy."

63.

When Monique and I limped home, she was bedridden and I had a large, competent nurse, Mrs. Sturges, to look after me around the clock. Don't mess with Mrs. Sturges—she's the boss. At first, neither Dad nor Monique were allowed to pick me up, bathe me in the kitchen sink, change my diapers, or tickle my feet to check out my Babinski. If they tried to sneak in a tickle, Mrs. Sturges glared at them like a Teutonic warrior about to fling a battle ax. In actuality, she was a gentle and very adept human being with a heart of gold, as compassionate as they come, a person who never spoke a harsh word to any of us.

At feeding time she carried me into the bedroom, placing me carefully in Monique's arms. My mother drowsed while I loaded up. When I finished suckling, Mrs. Sturges firmly pried me away again and Monique fell asleep.

My sleeping basket was located in the front room of our apartment. Mrs. Sturges bedded down on a cot beside me. She also cleaned, cooked, washed dishes, dusted rugs, polished silverware, watered the geraniums, and probably would have repainted the living room if we'd asked her to.

Monique remained weak and supine most of the time. Occasionally, she got up and essayed a few steps, then crashed again. Her heart did not feel great.

"You just relax, dear." Mrs. Sturges patted Monique's arm. "You have created a lovely child and you deserve to take it easy. Don't worry about a thing. Just remember that I'm on board this ship, and I have my hand on the tiller."

64.

I note that Goggie Davison paid for all my prenatal care, for the costs of my birth, for Mrs. Sturges, and for Monique's electrocardiogram and other doctor bills both before and after my arrival.

She was our financial guardian angel.

65.

Three weeks after my birth Monique was able to spend an hour or so on our backyard couch-swing, wrapped in a blanket, her head on a pillow, soaking up the sunshine. She felt so tired, so feeble: all of her body ached. Drowsing, she must have looked hauntingly beautiful and fragile. The quick shadows of flying birds streaked across her face.

Sometimes Mrs. Sturges sat in a chair by the swing, cuddling my sleepy body wrapped in a blanket against her bosom. She didn't try to keep up a chatter, or hum lullabies to me. Mostly, my nurse was quietly *there*, holding Monique's baby nearby, keeping my mom company so that every time Monique opened her eyes for a moment her baby was apparent and she could close her eyes again, reassured.

66.

Rodney Hadden made a house call. "Do not be active for a couple of months," he cautioned. Although Monique slowly grew strong enough to watch Mrs. Sturges bathing me and changing my diapers, she was not allowed to lift me or hold me herself except at feeding time. Otherwise, her hands remained crossed on her lap. She did not write letters or feel like reading a book. Her radio stayed tuned low to soft classical music. Occasionally, apprehensive for her friends and countrymen, she switched to a news station and followed Hitler's aerial blitz of London and the RAF's retaliation by bombing Berlin. Marshall Pétain had established a new French government at Vichy, collaborating with the Germans. The British navy destroyed the French fleet in Algeria so those ships could not be commandeered by the Nazis. Then Britain surrendered Somaliland to Italy, and Japanese soldiers occupied Shanghai—

Monique switched back to Mozart and Debussy.

67.

The first day of fall semester Monique said wistfully: "I can imagine how lively the grounds and the streets near the campus must be today. It seems funny not to see it with my own eyes, but I am no longer a carefree student's wife but the mother of a student's son with more important things to do. Don't misunderstand! I am still David's wife and plan to remain so! And I love being home with my baby."

That morning she had given me my first bath with her own hands. "I had watched the procedure several times already and, according to Mrs. Sturges who supervised, I did pretty well! I felt darned pleased and proud anyway, and Johnny was so sweet and good, not crying or fretting once. He didn't even drown!"

68.

During the last days of August Mrs. Sturges tendered Monique a warm and long-lasting embrace and tearfully abandoned her post at Dwight Way, leaving the new mother on her own five weeks after my arrival. By then my mom was stronger and glad to have me to herself. Monique laughed at her spells of clumsiness, cherishing difficult moments as well as happy times. In her letters she described me as an angel—"good as gold"—who rarely cried, soon developed a mischievous smile, and was always hungry. When Pop collapsed with yet another cold for a week, Monique was on top of things, caring for us both.

"I'm faster than a speedy bullet," she piped. "And able to bathe two men with a single splash."

69.

Sad to say, my dad lacked Monique's sangfroid and her sense of humor. "The advent of my son," as he put it, seemed to be a wake-up call that caused him to panic. Eleven days after my arrival he conveyed the thought to Grandpa that he might not become a professional zoologist, because he was now more inclined to a "non-professional" career. He might change his major from biology to Political Science since he had "more than myself to consider now." Like, for example, yours truly. And, lest we forget, his wife Monique, also. Pop added, "I believe that I am better fitted to be a salesman, a politician, a thief, or a lumberjack than I am to be a highly academic scientist."

He did not immediately metamorphose into a politician, a thief, or a lumberjack, however. He'd only been testing the waters, yet had decided not to do the crazy thing and jump in.

70.

But then Mamita and Ninon expressed a desire to visit Berkeley with Nito in tow. You're kidding! Nope, they feared that if Franco joined the Axis powers, Spain would be back at war and Nito, as a French citizen, would surely be drafted to fight for Marshall Henri Pétain's Vichy government that was in cahoots with the Nazis against the Allies. Not to be gross, but Pop needed three more adult residents of his four-room apartment on Dwight Way like he needed a broom handle up his rectum. And let's be straight: it wasn't *his* war. He didn't sign up for it. He wasn't responsible. He was not, repeat *not*, a French citizen. And his country wasn't at war, was it? So why should he be obligated to become involved?

David Nichols kept these negative feelings to himself. In his dreams, however, I'll bet Mamita appeared wearing a swastika armband and sporting a Hitler moustache. In other dreams Ninon probably showed up voluptuously naked . . . and brandishing a Tommy gun. And no doubt Nito materialized standing behind her wearing a tight red suit, with big horns on his head, a tail with an arrow point at the end of it, and miniature cloven hooves.

71.

In public, Pop claimed that he enjoyed watching Monique as a new mom. He considered her a natural at taking care of me. "She has absolute self-confidence in her own ability—something she did not have before Johnny's arrival. She bathes him and changes him without any trouble whatsoever and is just thrilled with the doing of it."

But with his course load and many other extracurricular activities, my father had difficulty taking care of his own obligations. In particular he concluded that it had become too much trouble to keep up his observations at the Aquatic Park.

"Sometimes Monique does the job for me," he said. "Always she goes over the results of the forty minute trip with me and works up the chart. I wouldn't let her do it and would be obliged to let the project drop except that she gets an awful lot of real solid enjoyment out of it."

That seems patronizing. Monique derived more than "solid enjoyment" from the Aquatic Park project. She no longer attended German classes at the university;

she had a full-time job taking care of me; and when my dad drove off on collecting trips Monique and I were never invited along. The sublime camping days of 1939 were over. Monique was not Dad's partner in science anymore, she was a housewife, a mother, a stay-at-home while Pop cavorted through the wilds with Frank Watson and Bob Storer and their other buddies researching birds, small mammals, and interesting roadkill.

So for Monique the daily census at the Aquatic Park remained a major connection to her husband, a way she might continue to share the naturalist life with him. As far as she was concerned they were still in it together. Partners. Monique had cast her lot with my dad's passion for the natural world, and it was her passion also, a visceral part of how they loved each other. And it would've been a terrible blow to have that important bond severed by the fact that they now had a baby.

One night in bed Pop offhandedly mentioned that the Aquatic Park project might have to be scrubbed. Without thinking, Monique reached over and grasped his nose, twisting it until he blurted, "*Ouch!*"

72.

Every time Mom and Dad attempted to have sex while I was napping or down for the night, I woke up and began gurgling and whimpering petulantly. Pop got out of bed and picked me up, and walked me around the small apartment singing *"Fais Dodo"* or "My Bonnie Lies Over the Ocean" until I went back to sleep. Then he very carefully returned me to my basket and slipped under the covers with Monique. They tried to be extra quiet, but the bed squeaked, and, sure enough, I'd commence my groggy fussbudget noises again. So Dad walked me around the apartment again. As Monique was too shy to expose herself unclothed like that, it was his job. Decades later Dad recalled that he often sang really nasty songs to me in a mellifluous tone, disguised as a lullaby, that knocked me out. His favorite was one he called "Dunderbeck." Officially, I think the title is "Johnny Vorbeck."

Oh Dunderbeck, oh Dunderbeck,
How could you be so mean?
We're sorry you invented
That horrid old machine.
The pussycats and longtail rats
Will nevermore be seen.
Because they're all ground up into
sausage meat
In Dunderbeck's machine.

And when I conked out they would try again.

However, inevitably, they fell victim to *coitus interruptus* once more.

In his old age, laughing at the memory, Pop told me, "For at least your first year it was almost impossible to get a piece of tail from your mother without waking you up. And I've held that against you ever since!"

73.

Then off he sped on another jaunt seventy miles north of Berkeley with twenty guys from the Grinnell Society. Their purpose? To search for tree mice. Among his collector friends were Frank Watson and Bob Storer. At one point Dad grabbed a female tree mouse that another fellow had knocked from a nest, and it bit him leaving four tiny puncture wounds at the tip of his finger. Fortunately, he did not land in the Intensive Care Unit of Alta Bates Hospital. Instead, he wound up at Spenger's Restaurant where Bob and Frank and the boys raised high their beer mugs and gave three cheers to the intrepid white hunter. Catching tree mice was David Nichols' version of shooting African rhinos or a charging water buffalo.

Trying not to be sarcastic, Monique carefully affixed a little Band-Aid onto the tip of his injured finger, then she kissed it to make it better.

74.

So my mom cared for Pop when he was sick, and she cared for me. My father claimed that, "Johnny and Monique are in fine condition largely due to the wonderful energy and care of the latter. The two of them fill the house with pleasantness."

Sad to say, it wasn't all roses for Monique. She continued battling those itchy "ringworms" which had now spread over most of her body. Her dermatologist ". . . burned them off with some sort of strong rays which act like a sunburn. I think I have got rid of them now, or just about. I have never had anything like it before and can't imagine how I caught this. I look like a stamp collection!"

75.

On fall evenings Pop listened to his shortwave radio, to programs from Europe in Russian and French, and to broadcasts from England, Canada, Australia. Monique did not often participate because of me, and because the news was never good. Germany bombed London daily. Japan had joined the Axis pact and invaded Indochina. Italy attacked Greece. At home, Roosevelt defeated Wendell Willkie for his third term as President. And, preparing for the possibility of war, the United States drew its first peacetime draft number while Nazi troops herded Warsaw's Jewish population into that city's ghetto.

The war had gotten to my old man. Prone to depression, his devotion to the house mouse laboratory waned, until abruptly the world's foremost authority on *Mus musculus* decided to abandon his wards. How come? Well, for starters his son, "a jolly little chap," had begun howling at 1:00 a.m. and taking so much of Monique's attention and affection (and costing a fortune into the bargain) that Dad's days had become seriously encumbered. And Frank Watson, busy courting Jean, the woman who would soon become his wife, was less available to wash mouse cages. And Bob Storer had too many irons in *his* fire. Hence, given the ordeal of now having a baby and more costs to take care of it, there existed not enough time or money to continue renting the mouse experiment space. So the surviving guys and gals were summarily put out of their misery and deposited at Berkeley's Museum of Vertebrate Zoology while I now began to rigorously serenade my folks after midnight with choking gurgles, obnoxious whining, chronic coughing, and, upon occasion, all out shrieking. The angry landlord banged on our wall.

Monique remained unfazed. She *loved* her sweet, adorable baby.

On the other hand, Dad could not quite believe that he had helped to create "this noisy little wretch."

76.

During the third week of November, Pop escaped my midnight disruptions by initiating another auto trip that covered 1300 miles over three days. He and a Dutch ornithologist pal, Joost ter Pelkwijk, drove to Yosemite, then into the San Joaquin Valley, then north to Sacramento and across the mountains to Reno, up to Pyramid Lake, then northwest to Susanville and across the mountains to Eureka on the ocean, and down the Redwood Highway to San Francisco.

During that odyssey Pop snapped a picture of Joost wearing a cowboy hat with a large tarantula spider on the front brim. I remember it from one of Dad's albums. A few years from now Joost was going to die in the battle of the Coral Sea and Pop would send a copy of the photograph to his family.

While they were gone Monique refused to miss a day at the Aquatic Park. Friends babysat me while she circled the lagoon taking names. There were so many different species and so many total birds now that the migrations were coming through. My mom really labored to list them in the natural history journal. Often she saw over thirty species and counted more than a thousand individual birds.

When my father returned from his globe-trotting, there was a freshly-baked chocolate cake waiting for him on the dining table. On a sheet of poster board propped up against a pile of books behind the cake Monique had painted a large fantastical raptor that held a dangling man the size of a mouse in its curved beak. An arrow pointing at the comical little captive had DAVE NICHOLS written at the end of its shaft. My mother enjoyed drawing and painting impressionistic outdoor landscapes, or funny people wearing fashionable clothes, or whimsical sailboats on the ocean with seagulls overhead and oddball fish bigger than the boats jumping out of the water. Her paintings were skillful even if childlike and all out of proportion. They were cartoons yet carefully designed and pretty, and they made you laugh. Their innocence was intoxicating.

77.

Come December, my parents mailed out a hundred and fifty Christmas greetings. Or, rather, Monique mailed them out. Their card was a photograph of an English sparrow with *Merry Christmas from Monique, Dave, and Johnny Nichols* scrawled by my mother across the back.

For the holidays, according to Monique, they had ". . . a small Christmas tree which is standing on the card table in the corner between Dave's desk and the front window. Below the tree, we have set up a little 'crèche' or manger which I got at Woolworth with little figures to represent the Nativity (some of them are made in Germany, others in Italy, and the rest in England! A peaceful gathering!) We have added a lot of black wood animals which Dave gave me in Paris so that our happy scene looks like a strange concoction of the birth of Christ and Noah's Ark! Two evenings ago we decorated the tree and Dave got some lovely miniature brass candlesticks with small birthday cake candles to brighten up our little crèche. It looks very sweet and we light it up every evening before going to bed and watch the candles until they go out one by one."

78.

The first week of January, 1941, my old man panicked. He was so overextended he could barely function. Life had him bowled over in a constant tizzy. He was taking care of all sorts of business except the business he should have been taking care of. Family stipends (from Grandmother Nichols, from Grammie and Grandpa, sometimes from Goggie Davison and even Mamita) were keeping his family alive, but he overspent the meager funds. He had a fragile constitution, a fragile wife, a new kid. You can't juggle sixteen balls when you should only be juggling five. According to Pop, he was running around ". . . like a squirrel with his nuts in a vice." He felt antsy, torn, guilty, besieged, overburdened, snowed under. He said, "I have to start increasing the family's earning power." *Seriously.* He was always short of money. Unfortunately, "Every time I sit at my desk the telephone rings, the baby cries, my tooth aches, someone drops in to call, or the tailor drops in to collect a bill. I have been interrupted out of my work by innumerable details which are not more than comedy in the telling, but which just smother accomplishment in actuality." Over Christmas vacation he had "carried on the Aquatic Park project, washed the dishes after every meal that I am at home, I have gone to the movies six or seven times, I have gone skating several times, I have swept the house from time to time, I have read the constitution of the Soviet Union, United States, and France, I have eaten Kangaroo Rats, I have sung French, Russian, British and American folk songs for guests, I cooked two ducks on Christmas eve, I have written two or three professional letters not requiring much thought and a few social letters requiring a lot of thought, I have had a tooth pulled, I have had teeth filled, I have had many headaches, toothaches, and chest pains throughout the rainy season . . ."

The letter blathered on kvetching about his "hodgepodge of inconsequential and varied activities" for five more typed pages. It was all crazy. Yet despite the myriad helter-skelter commitments driving him nuts, Pop was about to become the (volunteer) editor of the Golden Gate Audubon Association's publication, *The Gull.* And he and his wife had signed up for Esperanto lessons. Like a man on a suicide mission, my father couldn't stop himself. When you had a baby everything changed. Which way should he jump? And how high? Should he sprout wings like a marsh hawk and commence quartering the Berkeley mud flats for clams, crabs, and sanderlings to bring home for the family dinner? Of course, no matter what he decided, his plans could instantly be torn asunder by the accelerating world events. Every night he followed the bloodbath on his shortwave radio until Monique begged him to come to bed, hold her in his arms, and make love with her if he could.

79.

Next day Dad fired off a more desperate note to his folks, alerting them that he planned to drive east alone immediately, in his friend Martha Boyden's car, to consult with his family for answers to "various little personal problems." He sounded extra frantic, telling

Grammie that Monique had okayed the trip, backing him one hundred percent. Dad believed his problems would ". . . lose their troublesome aspect when commented upon by the family."

"This trip is very sudden," Monique admitted to Grammie, "and I can't quite believe it yet. I know how you must all feel and hope you are not worrying. There is nothing wrong, nothing exciting, no new baby in the offing either! For quite some time Dave has had things on his mind which he wanted to talk over with you and Dad. No great idea, just a lot of everyday things. He also misses you a great deal and has wanted to see you very much."

She concluded: "And so, here I am, a widow again for some time. I shall miss Dave, but am so happy to think of his joy in being with you that I won't miss him too much. Also, I still have a man left, although he is rather tiny!"

80.
Martha Boyden's car made it across country. While my dad conferred with his family at their year-round Garden City home on Long Island, Monique continued her daily Aquatic Park lists. Some days she was accompanied by Bob Storer and Frank Watson, who treated her with kindness and humor. They knew something

was out of whack with my dad, yet never brought it up with Monique. Often I came along to the park and the lads made faces at me, tickled my chin, or bounced me on their knees to shut me up. The weather was sunny, breezy, nice.

Dad received a letter from Monique each day. I don't know if he wrote her back. She kept extra busy at home feeding me and bathing me and pushing me in a stroller. She cleaned out the Dwight Way closets, shelves, and drawers, and stuck the family photographs in albums, and finished filing away my dad's large correspondence which had been stacked in cardboard boxes. Time permitting, she also skated with friends, proud of her new skills on ice.

Monique waxed elegiac with Grammie. "I can see you all around the fireplace, talking or reading aloud or just sitting. Dad is adding more little black marks on the mantle front with his feet. Patty is snoring on her rug. Mother has her special cap on and is sucking a cough drop. I don't know what Floyd and Dave are doing but I am sure John has closed the door and is playing the piano in the next room. Such a familiar picture. I feel right there with you."

My mom and her rose-colored glasses.

81.

Pop's train bringing him back alive arrived in Berkeley just in time for Monique's twenty-sixth birthday on January 20. The moment she recognized David at the station, my mother was struck by his improved mien. He looked so much better than when he'd left. They dined together at Capri, an Italian restaurant in Oakland, then saw a movie, *The Santa Fe Trail.* Afterward, at Trader Vic's on the bay, they downed two drinks and danced. Later, they drove over to San Francisco and visited the Rainbow Room at the top of the Mark Hopkins Hotel simply to enjoy the view of the city below. As Dad toasted Monique with champagne he mentioned that he might quit school and move the family to New Orleans.

He *what?*

Yes, her "jaw dropped" and she couldn't help but exclaim, "*As tu perdu ta raison?*"

We did *not* move to New Orleans.

82.

Toward the end of January, Dad matriculated back to school, though his heart wasn't really in it. Yet if he quit now, what was the point of all the effort he'd put into his education since 1938? At twenty-four years of age he didn't even have a high school diploma, let alone a university degree. At the same time his family was barely surviving on the monthly allowance from Grammie and Grandpa and other family members. To put it concisely, we were living about a block away from the poorhouse. So what had the old man been thinking when he boarded an ocean liner in October of 1938 to cross the sea and win back his fiancée, marry her, then have a child when he had not a penny in his pocket, no job, and the mindset of a ten-year-old?

Pop had one foot in academia, one foot out. But it was all absurd. Of course, whatever he might choose to do (short of moving to New Orleans!), Monique supported him wholly, no questions asked. He was her man, she his wife, and she loved him without reservations. She believed in his genius. Her good nature flooded our small apartment. My innocent *and* perceptive mother rarely complained. I doubt she was a simpleton. I would place her as the first, and also the last, woman in my father's life journey to give him unconditional affection, no strings attached. His complex emotional and intellectual personality was often baffled by her sunny disposition and unfaltering loyalty.

83.

Monique had her hands full just taking care of yours truly. Every time I sprung a bad rash, it cost money. Every time I needed an inoculation, it cost money. Every time I got a sore throat or croup, it cost money. My illness expenses were sucking us toward financial annihilation.

So Dad began an independent service offering translations of zoological material in Russian, French, Spanish, Portuguese, and Italian. He hoped to earn a few dollars independent of the east coast relatives. Monique was his partner because she could do the Spanish, Portuguese, Italian and French. Dad's initial job concerned an entry for peregrine falcons taken from an old Russian encyclopedia. I think he was paid ten dollars.

That was a start. It was also pathetic. He might as well have created an independent service offering cruelty-free whale blubber to vegetarian restaurants if any had existed back then. The truth is Pop couldn't earn his way out of a paper bag. David Nichols possessed about as much financial savvy as "a month-old baby with diphtheria." His chances of becoming rich some day were "one in a trillion." These were *his* assessments of himself, not mine or Monique's.

84.
Still, we mustn't forget they had fun. At the
completion of his zoology field trips, Dad sometimes
brought friends home for lunch or supper. Monique
enjoyed talking science with them, eager for the
connection. She sorely missed the northern California
and Nevada birding expeditions with her husband, yet
never uttered a contrary peep. One night, after my folks
hired a babysitter and attended a Cooper Club meeting
together, they went for beer and snacks at Spenger's
Restaurant with fellow ornithologists. Everyone at the
table began imitating bird calls. Monique derived such
a kick from that, happy to be included. She could do
a slew of bird calls pretty well herself, among them a
hermit thrush, a ruby-crowned kinglet, a common crow.
She remembered standing under trees at the William
Floyd estate while Dad called in those noisy black birds.
   Diners at the other tables glanced up with amusement.
Hey, who was that pretty woman over there cawing like a crow?
   I'd like to think that the waiter approached their
noisy gang, saying, "No more wine for you folks. And
no more beer, either."

85.

On February 9, 1941, Monique reported to her in-laws: "We are all well and *very* happy. I have calculated that, so far, I have fed Johnny over 700 times! His meals seem to come around pretty often, especially when I have a busy day! But it is so much fun and it gives me so much pride and satisfaction to see him eat well or to manage to make him eat spinach."

My dad's side of their story? "Living in an apartment with a baby is beginning to be something of a burden on M. The increased use of gas, water, electricity, and garbage as well as midnight crying are also beginning to be a little bit of a burden on the landlord. The landlord's family is also beginning to be a little bit of a burden on me. All things considered, then, I started sounding out the various house possibilities . . ."

Ziiiip! Suddenly we moved into a house, a *real* house, on 1710 Grant Street in Berkeley. Oopsy-daisy. *That* was a big upheaval. The rent? $45.00 a month. Could we afford it? Who cared?—Dad was adamant. The house had an upstairs and a downstairs, large rooms, big closets, *space*. No landlord's apartment stood on the other side of our walls. We had *privacy*. David and Monique bought a few pieces of secondhand furniture and a used stove. My mother acquired a

John Treadwell Nichols and John Treadwell Nichols II, Berkeley, 1941.
(I.E.: Grandpa and Johnny.)

battered Chesterfield for seven dollars at the Red Cross store. She planned her housework carefully so as not to climb up and down the stairs too often. Her heart couldn't take that. But if the climb left her breathless, she rarely let on. Monique rested every couple of steps and switched me from one hip to the other. My father never noticed.

His desire was, "I just want to have a home of my own—I just want to sun Johnny in my back yard and cut a little grass on Saturday afternoons."

Then abruptly he quit his classes at UC Berkeley, abandoned science as a career, and began job hunting in San Francisco. It was high time he stormed the ramparts of monotonous working class travail, locked on his leg irons among the hoi polloi, and became a reliable family man.

86.

Dad attended a commercial school and a night school many hours a week, learning to type in order to better land viable employment. At home he typed and typed, practicing. He was driven. I fell asleep listening to his tapping; I awoke to his tap tap tap. His goal was to reach seventy words per minute. So he practiced and practiced and practiced. Looking at their natural history journal I see that Monique now appeared more often than Pop at the Aquatic Park to keep up their bird observations. Obviously, she was determined not to let them die.

Three days a week my father gave private Russian lessons to members of Berkeley's Museum of Vertebrate Zoology. Nobody paid him, but it was good practice. He and Monique dropped the Esperanto classes they had signed up for only a few weeks earlier. They had no time for chess games anymore. Having a child was expensive. And exhausting. It generated perpetual crises.

For example: "The little imp tried to scratch my eye out," Monique said. "I was giving him his bath, and, as always, he kicked and waved his hands to try to prevent me from washing his face. It's really a game, but this time one of his fingers got me in the left eye and the nail scratched it. I know those things can be nasty so I went immediately to see the oculist who took care of it, put a bandage on it, and told me I was lucky it hadn't been deeper. So up until recently, I have looked like a pirate with a black patch over my eye! Johnny thought it was all very funny."

But it caused more doctor bills.

87.

My old man couldn't help himself—he groused to his parents about those doctor bills. His outlook was grim. In one letter he thanked Grammie for her monthly allowance, then grumbled about his rent, utilities, and food bills, griped about his chest colds and dental problems, and, with a flourish, painted this scenario of his personal financial situation:

"If Monique gets scarlet fever, all my monetary reserve is wiped out like spit in the ocean. If Johnny gets it at the same time, I take my place behind the eight ball. From that time on I would have about as much choice about my future as a bug in fly syrup."

88.

And, just to keep Monique on her toes, I almost froze to death from throwing off my blankets at night. "His little hands are like icicles in the morning," she worried. My mom bought me some Dr. Denton durable footed pajamas with a flap in back (the "drop seat"), "made to withstand wear and tear by rollicksome children" the ads asserted. The pajamas vaunted flexible rubber buttons and "extra heavy romper feet," apparently just what I needed.

When fully awake I wriggled, kicked, rocked and rolled. "Promise not to tell outsiders," Monique confided to Grammie, "and I'll tell you a bad thing I did. I left him on our bed for a second the other evening while getting a diaper and the next thing I knew, I heard a thud and he was on the floor. I never was so scared in all my life. Luckily, he had been on his tummy and slid off the edge, gripping the bed spread so that his fall was slight and he didn't get hurt at all."

89.

But the true fact of the matter, to Monique's thinking, was that Johnny "is more fun every day. Sometimes, in the late afternoon when he is kicking and playing on a blanket on the floor of the parlor and Dave is working at his desk, Johnny goes through elaborate gestures and loud shouts to attract Dave's attention. And when Dave looks around and smiles at him, then his joy is complete."

Even though I was not yet a year old, apparently I sat up quite well during meals. "He has developed the most amusing pose, raising himself on his side with his head on his hand and elbow. In his long nightie, he thus looks like a Roman emperor at table!"

And my eyes were an amazing color. "Everyone tells us they are the bluest eyes they have ever seen. Not

---

light blue, but very dark, almost purple at times. He knows how to use them too and, although he has not learned to wink yet, he seems to flirt with them very much!"

On another occasion she said, "He played peekaboo with me yesterday, pulling covers over his head, then down, then up again, etc. He sleeps all morning after his bath and is awake most of the afternoon but plays quietly by himself. I don't want to spoil him but oh, he is such a good baby. It makes me sick to think you and my family can't see him now."

90.

A large back yard at the Grant Street house was clogged with weeds and singing birds. My folks started cleaning it up. They would shortly plant a fine garden, and they constructed a bird blind at the far end from which my father took photographs. The sun came out. Life was hopeful. They felt they were creating a *home*. Dad raised a fence around the back yard and painted it with Monique's help. From a nearby peach tree curious bushtits observed this operation. Pop leveraged up a tall pole for his shortwave radio antenna; broadcasts he continued to monitor originated from Moscow, Paris, London, Australia. A stickler for the correct hour, minute, and second, he always set his watch by

Greenwich Mean Time.

In a letter to a friend Monique explained that she now inhabited a "big old house with lots of room and almost no furniture." She confessed, "Our household is by no means a neat, well regulated one with a number of books, papers, etc. always lying around and people and friends dropping in at all hours and meals eaten at crazy hours. But we have such a good time and such a happy life."

Friends came to tea, to dinner, to Grinnell Society and Slavic Club and Cooper Club get-togethers. They arrived from distant cities, often exhausted, and spent the night. They came lugging their babies in baskets. Near strangers appeared for lunch and tarried all day, chatting. On a typical afternoon, Barbara May dropped by with her four-month-old baby. Then Virginia Olney rang the doorbell. Barbara left, and Ed Olney came to fetch his new wife about the hour Pop reached home, so Virginia and Ed were persuaded to stay for supper. Virginia and Monique planned to sponsor a dinner for some Grinnell Society bigwigs, a dinner they pulled off with great aplomb using a card table and the corner of two desks at 1710 Grant Street.

"It was a great success," Monique bragged. "At one point Johnny started showing off his energetic kicking and grunting abilities and we almost died from laughing. He was like a tiny little circus clown who'd had too much to drink!"

91.

When Grandpa stepped off the train for a short visit, he and I took to each other instantly. I camped on his lap and twisted his nose and probably tried to yank away his pipe or cram it down his throat. Onlookers chuckled. I have a picture of him holding me in his arms, awkwardly, sort of laughing, and I am cackling at the camera. Grandpa was six-foot-three, "lanky and taciturn with a wry sense of humor," always wreathed in tobacco smoke and wearing his eternally rumpled blue serge suit. He thought that Johnny "looks upon me as a punching bag." Pop and his old man went to the Aquatic Park, talking birds nonstop as they performed the daily census. On their second visit to the lagoon they invited Monique along and a neighbor took care of me. My mother and Grandpa were kindred souls, truly attached to each other. Grandpa never embraced women, he was too formal and shy for that. But if anybody loved Monique right to the bottom of their soul it was John Treadwell Nichols. I know he would never have said "I love you," that was not his style. Yet he and my mom understood each other at a profound and unspoken level. She was so proud to identify birds on the water while standing beside Grandpa at the Aquatic Park, and to give him correctly their Latin names.

Monique wept on the evening Grandpa departed in a Pullman car headed back east to Garden City, and, just like in the movies, she waved goodbye until the train was out of sight.

92.

Then this sad thing happened.

Dad was so busy attempting to find a job that he flat out gave up on the Aquatic Park census taking. He had lost the strength and the willpower to continue that daily chore. So he just bagged it. But Monique could not bear to let the project drop. And, from March 6 to March 18, she completed the Aquatic Park bird census by herself. She visited the park alone, scoping the birds and writing down her observations. She was happy to see a robin, only the second one they'd spied at the park over the past eleven months. Monique arrived at the lagoon between 6:00 and 6:30 a.m., meaning Pop stayed at home with me practicing his typing during her absence. He was approaching seventy words per minute.

Among the birds recorded by Monique on her final day were a common loon, white-winged scoters, western gulls, an American pipit, and a few white-crowned sparrows. The last bird on Monique's list was a solitary

Melospiza melodia, a song sparrow.

Then she was forced to give up the Aquatic Park project my parents had sustained for almost a year. With that, their natural history journals ended, extinguishing what had been a very bright light in Monique's world.

93.

Almost the following day, Pop landed a job with the American-Hawaiian Steamship Company on the San Francisco docks. Thank *you*. His first day of work he boarded a train for the city at 7:07 a.m. He was both agonized and relieved to abandon his studies. Longshoremen were a far cry from his academic colleagues. After a couple of weeks, in a letter to Grandpa, he had this to say about the steamship business. "Things are active on the piers. People are rough, good-hearted, self-centered, hard working, and dumb. One can understand wars and politics better by watching and listening to them than one can by watching the flabby, flannell-mouthed, red-lipped, waggling head of an academic man. In comparison with university men the pier-men are restful. Their anger, jealousy, pride, friendship, jokes, tears, and laughter are understandable. The nastiness washes out with the night fog. Their jokes soften their jealousies. All their emotions are simple in comparison with the balanced, festering, complicated, amplified or suppressed, dilly-dally emotions of academicians. Then there are stevedores who stand out for their fine values just as there are good professors."

A week later my dad sold the Grease Pig because it was costing too much, and that ended another era. Pop was beginning to take charge of things. The war was closing in on us, he could feel its pressure. The British and the free French under de Gaulle were winning in Libya. Martial law had been declared in Belgium to stop anti-Nazi riots. And under Japanese orders France had ceded parts of Laos and Cambodia to Thailand. The United States didn't like that. So despite landing a job, David Nichols brooded about what could happen next to upset his apple cart.

He did not have to wait long.

PART FOUR

Mamita and Johnny, Berkeley, 1941.

94.

Monique's little brother Nito set sail for America on June 17, 1941. He was approaching his seventeenth birthday. Mamita wrote that she and Ninon had vacillated about departing also. Spain was scrambling to avoid more battles as Franco maneuvered to placate Hitler and Mussolini while steering clear of their war. If the Spanish dictator joined the Axis powers, Nito would likely be drafted into the French Vichy army and wind up fighting against the Allies. Hence, it was prudent for him to leave Barcelona, join us in Berkeley, and enter the university here to receive an education commensurate with his remarkable academic capabilities.

Monique was apprehensive. "I certainly hope nothing happens but feel uneasy as I don't see how Spain can prevent being engulfed by Hitler too."

My father dreaded Nito's arrival. He dreaded the loss of privacy. He dreaded another human being to feed. "I finally get myself a damn job and now look what's happening." Monique had become totally preoccupied with Johnny, and Pop felt left out in the rain. How much further would he recede with Nito around? Already his wife and child had cost him his college education. And now the European war that his own country wasn't even involved in was going to take him farther away from his wife. Nito's presence would change the entire atmosphere of 1710 Grant Street, it would be an enormous intrusion on top of the baby's intrusion. And if Mamita and Ninon followed Nito to Berkeley—?

Dad kept everything inside. On the outside he smiled and joked and pandered and was cordial, and he lied through his teeth when people asked him how he felt. My father was charismatic. His energy was so *positive*. When he played his guitar and sang bawdy songs he shone like a star. He *was* a star. Even when Monique cuddled him in bed and gently hinted for the truth, he kissed her and insisted that everything was "copacetic" and "hunky-dory," even though, by a long shot, it wasn't. Pop was like a walking time bomb dressed up to resemble an articulate intellectual bon vivant . . . secretly dogged by depression, tension, fear of failure, insecurity. And guilt. I mean: What right did he have to resent his wife's family's dilemma, their lives torn apart by a ghastly conflict? Although Monique understood his stress and resentment, she was reluctant to force those things out of him. My mom harassed nobody.

95.

Nito's train chuffed into the Berkeley station. He was tall, handsome, a phenomenal scholar, and very introverted, almost pathologically shy. Also fluent in French, Spanish, German, English. "He plays the piano beautifully," my father said. "He gives our place a very festive air by playing folk songs from the Latin countries as well as many of the world's best classics."

Yet what endeared Nito immediately to my dad was his skill and enthusiasm as a lepidopterist. Pop's new boarder had a fanatical interest in butterflies and the natural world they occupy. And next thing you know, Nito and Dad were wandering around the Grant Street back yard snagging pretty insects from the air with filmy white nets that Nito had procured. And fairly soon my mother was out there with them catching admirals, painted ladies, mourning cloaks, and grasshoppers. She claimed, "I feel like we're in a movie about little Swiss kids dancing to celebrate their neutrality."

96.

Then Monique got really sick two weeks after Nito joined us. I don't know what happened to her, but it shook up the family. Dad's correspondence with his parents, often bold and funny, and, on the surface, candid, was also guarded, evasive, *opaque*, especially on this topic. I did not read his letters to Grammie and Grandpa revealing Monique's illness until over a decade after Pop's death. He certainly never mentioned that particular health crisis to me while he was alive.

To Grammie on July 19 he said, "Monique begs to be forgiven for not writing of late. Her gizzard is a bit disorganized. She is going to the hospital this evening to have it straightened out by a very minor operation. I think she will probably rest up in the hospital for five or six days. The woman who will take care of Johnny in Monique's absence is strong and agreeable."

And—?

And six days later, on July 25, he told Grandpa at the museum that everything was beginning to quiet down in his household now. "Nito is falling into the traces as an errand boy; Mrs. Vierra (practical nurse) is doing the work of the house and nursing Monique rather well; Monique is still in bed. This set-up will probably last until Tuesday or Wednesday of next week."

97.

His words to Grammie twenty-four hours later revealed: "I have been drinking acrid tea for the past few days. Although Monique is getting better and better she is still weak—still in bed—and easily fatigued.

"Data accumulated during the past few days indicate the necessity of taking her heart trouble more seriously than I have up until now. Moves must be made to avoid future bad troubles. Dr. Hadden advises eliminating stair climbing (for always, for good). I concur in his advice.

"This means moving to a one-floor house, or building here a playroom-closet-bath-toilet-storeroom affair in which the bulk of Johnny's, Monique's, and my daily life could be carried on so Monique would not have to use the stairs. Either solution is distasteful but my decision will probably be reached in the course of the next month."

However, at the present moment house-hunting would put Monique back in the hospital. Even worrying about the matter served "to pull her down a notch or two."

98.

On July 28 Monique was still in bed, with orders to try getting up and going to the bathroom that evening. Dad had already conferred with his landlord to see if the downstairs might be fixed up so my mom would not have to climb the stairs anymore. The landlord said he wouldn't invest *his* money in the project. Dad

seriously contemplated a move to a one-story rental.
Few were available, however. With war becoming more
imminent, either in Europe or against Japan, a defense
industry boom and naval contracts had locked up Bay
Area housing.

My father did not care to renovate the downstairs at
1710 Grant Street unless he owned the house. So the
landlord raised the required down payment from $500
to $750. Dad figured he had three choices. 1.) Get the
hell out. 2.) Buy at the landlord's price. 3.) Or continue
to rent, probably at a higher cost.

He concluded this cheery note by saying, "My landlord is not to be trusted. I am obliged to assume that
he is doing everything dishonestly."

99.

But what was *wrong* with Monique?

Pop refused to elucidate, in a letter, the "very minor
operation" and its aftermath. "Her gizzard is a bit
disorganized?" What did *that* mean? His August third
mailing to Grandpa admitted, "It is going to grieve
both of us very much to have to leave this place which
has seemed just about ideal; but I guess we will have
to face the facts sooner or later and pull out. I am
also in doubt about what I will use for money in re-
establishing myself."

In the meantime he carried Monique upstairs whenever she needed or wanted to go there.

100.

At this point Grammie sent him a letter that must have been rife with pointed questions and unwelcome advice. Though I have never seen Grammie's document, I do have a carbon copy of Dad's reply. His three-page typed letter on August 5, 1941, is elaborate, tense, aggravated, and aggravating. Thanking his mother for her sympathy, he expressed dismay that they could not talk things over, face-to-face, more often. He apologized for his incomplete reporting of "the ins and outs of our existence," because, sadly, "being candid in correspondence" was difficult. No doubt his letters to Grammie had oversimplified Monique's situation. Health problems composed only a small portion of their present difficulties, he admitted, but "It is distasteful to us to put the intimate details of our insides on paper. It seems to contribute to hypochondria."

In short: "I don't think you should approach the dangerous province of giving medical advice about my family."

101.

Pop would not have picked up a telephone for all the money in China, which is about what a long distance phone call to New York back then would have cost.

102.

And despite a thorough search of my dad's archives and of materials at the William Floyd estate, I can locate no correspondence that fully explains Monique's "very minor operation" that July, or its problematic aftermath. Monique herself kept mum on the subject. The only thing she ever said in a letter was, "The last month certainly has been full of all kinds of things, both good and bad. After the operation, my heart didn't react very well or reacted too much." Period. End of story. No elaboration. And her letter writing to Grammie and Grandpa from this moment on really tailed off.

To me, the most logical conclusion I can reach is that my mother, pregnant, may have been anesthetized for an abortion and her heart went into alarming atrial fibrillation. I get the impression Dr. Hadden was very progressive, probably pro-choice long before choice existed legally, and most likely he would have approved of the procedure.

But I will never know what really took place, although I realize, in hindsight, that it foretold what would happen next.

103.

Dad's following letters to Grammie and Grandpa were also gloomy. At work he'd been transferred from Pier 26 to an uptown office, and the strain of learning about a whole new set of activities bugged him. As American relations with Japan grew worse, company operations changed on a daily basis. The U.S. government had taken over fifty percent of American-Hawaiian's ships. We had frozen Japanese assets, withheld oil from Japanese tankers, and warned Tokyo not to interfere with American shipping in the Pacific.

Then look at the grotesque European war. Hitler had invaded the Soviet Union, expanding his murderous swath to Novgorod, Bialystok, Minsk, Smolensk, and all across the Ukraine, eager to conquer Kiev, Leningrad, Moscow, Stalingrad. How could the United States keep out of it? At home Pop turned on his shortwave radio with serious trepidation.

104.

Meanwhile, Nito registered for the fall semester at
UC Berkeley, taking three courses in mathematics and
two in physics. He studied around the clock, having
difficulty with math problems in English, yet he was
adroit and caught on quickly. Quiet and unobtrusive,
he played piano and helped cook meals and cleaned the
house. They all spoke French together. Sometimes Nito
and Monique conversed with each other in Spanish,
although never in front of Dad: they abhorred being
rude.

For the first time ever my mom and her little brother
had intimate talks, one-on-one. Their age difference,
childhood separations, and Monique's travels meant
they'd grown up as strangers. But now that changed.
Monique learned that Nito was a considerate, gentle,
and loving boy. Nito discovered that his big sister was a
compassionate live wire with a heart as big as the ocean.
They were startled, and proud, at this late date, to fall in
love with each others' humanity.

105.

Re Nito, though, Grammie couldn't keep her mouth
shut. In an ill-advised letter she suggested to Pop that

caring for Nito was putting undue stress on Monique and him. Maybe so, yet my father replied in a letter that I consider courageous and beautiful: "I must put you at rest on one point. He [Nito] is the most willing helper about the house that there could be. Without him things would have been much more difficult during Monique's illness. What to do with Nito and his family as time progresses? Mix the multitudinous practical problems of every day life with the opportunity to play a vital role in one of the most moving tragedies life can produce— being driven away from home, to be a refugee. This mixture will produce a puzzling juxtaposition of ideas and emotions. Think of the experience I am gaining by taking care of Nito. Calculate the importance of the next six months to him: what will it mean in his life? No words can describe the intense excitement, the wonder, the prayers, the longings, the flashes of devotion, friendship, disgust, reluctance, dismay, and determination which are exchanged between the three of us every day. Here is a household of cultured, sensitive, widely experienced young people working out their problems together—not always in harmony— always with faith in themselves. To decide that this or that will be done with Nito is far beyond the reach of cold intellect. We'll just take it easy—do the best we can—not tire ourselves out by swimming against the undertow—and adjust the details as they come up. I

doubt that any of us would care to part company—
more especially in difficult times."

106.

Hello? Johnny to the Literary Galaxy? Let's not forget about *me* during all this grownup *Sturm und Drang!*
I've been off stage too long, absent from everyone's
letters. So I need to interject here, at least briefly, that I
helped myself out learning to walk by pushing a small
table around our living room.

Let Monique paint the picture: "Whenever he comes
up against something and cannot go farther, he reverses
the process and starts pulling the table until he is clear
of the object and can push on again. This same small
table, (which I purchased for 50c second-hand) is a
source of continued joy to him. I can turn it upside
down and sit him in it and make a little house of his
own in that way. Johnny must be getting more teeth.
At least he has never drooled so much. I actually have
to mop up pools of saliva where he has stood on the
floor for some length of time."

107.

At work Pop became even more disgruntled. Everything was unsettled in the shipping business. "I may

get pitched out on my ass anytime." From his office he constantly observed the boats on San Francisco Bay. Navy light cruisers plowed in and out of the harbor. They were painted dark colors so as not to "show up against the shore line." Because America had frozen Japanese assets, Japanese freighters were stranded in the bay. "I wonder what they are waiting for?" On the government launch pier Dad noticed that U.S. customs agents severely processed Japanese citizens about to board ships for a return home. They were patted down thoroughly and then had billy clubs tapped rudely against their buttocks. Destroyers appeared regularly. "Now and then a battle ship comes in for a few days and sails off again in the night time."

Monique registered as an alien and was duly fingerprinted. My father was called to the office on Saturdays, working overtime. Something major and ominous was brewing. The newspapers and his shortwave radio kept him informed. Sort of. Clearly, though, much of the real news was being censored.

He and Monique didn't talk about these things very much. They preferred being "cheerful."

108.

However, insult to injury, our household now anticipated the arrival of Mamita and Ninon. I can imagine

Nito and Johnny, Berkeley, 1941

Pop slamming the heel of his hand so hard against the side of his head that he bumped into a wall and hurt his elbow! Yes, Mamita and Ninon had decided to flee the Spanish turmoil and hunker down in America . . . at 1710 Grant Street with Dad, Monique, yours truly, and Nito. Spain had sent a division to fight alongside the Germans at Leningrad, so it looked as if any day now Franco might declare for the Axis powers and fully enter the war.

The old man could not believe it. Almost four years

earlier he'd fallen in love with a wonderful French girl with whom he had planned to spend the rest of his days, shored up by her blithe spirit and awe of nature, her domestic skills and unfettered devotion to his career ambitions. She had been so strong and lively, so humorous, playful, and understanding—a perfect mate. Yet nowadays, barely a blink in time later, he was financially strapped, sleepless because of a noisy child, bereft of his education, caretaking his fragile wife and her little brother, and about to be inundated by his more arrogant in-laws. Right now those in-laws were on a boat somewhere crossing the Atlantic. And his own life was about to go down the crapper once more.

Dad informed Grandpa: "No news to date from the Roberts that are supposed to be on the ocean. We hope that the Gestapo didn't stick them in the clink before they could fly the coop."

Yet wouldn't *that* have been providential?

109.

Whoosh! Mamita and Ninon arrived in Berkeley on September 23, 1941. This created a clamor. How did they wrangle so many suitcases across the ocean to the United States in the middle of a war? They settled in at 1710 Grant Street with much commentary upon the dearth of rugs, unsatisfactory curtains, the lack of a bannister on the stairs, and the weird bathroom toilet paper dispensers. And how come there's no *bidet*? For how long will their visit be? They don't know, their daily lives have become total improvisation. Confusion reigned. War is hell. *"On est foutu!"* Mamita needed to see a *peluquera* immediately to have her hair retinted blue. Ninon could not believe Monique had no emery boards or fingernail polish. *"Tu es dingue, toi."* Her own bottles never made it through customs. And her only pair of stockings had a run in one leg, but was it really true that her big sister possessed none of that glamour-girl stuff she could borrow? *"Quelle horreur!"* They laughed and hugged, happy to be together again.

110.
Monique was super elated to have all her family on board, relatives whom she hadn't seen since her Paris wedding almost three years earlier. She had neatened up papers, books, and general clutter around the house. Mamita was not a fan of clutter. A maid, Callie Washington, had helped scrub and wax the floors, dust the rugs, clean the toilet and windows. Nito and my dad got haircuts. Gritting his teeth in frustration, Pop had even organized into neat piles all the translating materials scattered across his desk.
Myself, I was truly good-natured and harmless until

waking everybody at 3:00 a.m. with the arrival of my new teething problems. Monique manifested colds weekly but managed to cook, sew, wash, and sweep the floor repeatedly. Dad jumped onto the train for San Francisco each morning at 6:37 a.m. now, overjoyed to escape. He was *"l'homme invisible,"* according to Ninon. The invisible man. Nito remained withdrawn, extra polite, and very studious, attending classes and studying around the clock—he was not present for many family activities either. Ninon called him, *"Notre petit moine."* Our little monk. "He hates us because he's so smart and we're such dilettantes." Ninon herself was gorgeous, sickly, self-absorbed, irascible, sarcastic, fun-loving, and lazy. She had nothing to *do* and stated often, *"Je creve d'ennui."* She was bored to tears. Mamita, a *grande dame* living in exile far outside her milieu and comfort zone, couldn't just sit around twiddling her thumbs. Off to the library she raced beside my mom and me in a taxi, returning with: a couple of mysteries; Hemingway's *For Whom the Bell Tolls*; and a history of the North Pole's exploration by dirigible. Then away to the movies Mamita and Ninon went accompanied by Monique, taking in *Citizen Kane*, *The Maltese Falcon*, *The Great Dictator*, and *Gone with the Wind*, the original English version of it they hadn't seen before. Nito and my dad shared the babysitting chores while Nito tried to study for multiple classes, and Pop kept translating his

Russian articles. I had to raise my screechy voice quite often in hopes of shocking those two bookworms into looking after my toddler needs.

111.

Mamita must have tickled my chin and spoken to me in French expecting me to respond in French. That was important to her. But I was scarcely over a year old.

A search through all my photo albums reveals that I have one picture of myself with Mamita in Berkeley. A black and white snapshot. I *think* I am about sixteen months old. My grandmother is sort of squatting on the sidewalk at my level sniffing a flower that I have picked from a bush I'm standing beside. Mamita's right hand steadies my wrist so that she can inhale odor from the flower. My left hand, stretched backwards, is clutching a bunch of leaves, perhaps for balance. Mamita wears a gray flannel jacket and gray flannel pleated skirt. I am attired in a long-sleeved jersey, short dark pants, white socks and white kiddie shoes. I have chubby knees with dimples, and I am smiling and very interested in Mamita's interaction with the vegetation I am proffering her. Mamita's hair is cut short and waved. I assume it was tinted blue. She does look the matron. We both have Le Braz noses, fat cheeks, and big ears with oversized earlobes.

Obviously, I am "*adorable*." In French you pronounce that "*Ah-door-AH-bluh*."

112.

Mamita's finances were dicey and she discussed them a lot with my father. Like it or not, he was her *consiglieri* in America. Lucky him. Every other morning Dad fired off another letter to Grandpa at the New York Museum of Natural History trying to explain Mamita's finances. She had asked him to set up bank accounts fronting for her because she was not a United States' citizen. Pop wanted Grandpa to have a tally of these dealings in case the FBI sought to bust him for collaborating with an "alien." He was afraid Mamita would force him to break a dozen American laws at a time when violating certain legal directives by colluding with a foreigner might be frowned upon as unpatriotic, perhaps even treasonous. Especially with a French national whose Vichy government was collaborating with the Nazis.

Expecting to receive three grand a year as a U.S. resident, Mamita offered Pop and Monique $70.00 a month to cover her, Ninon, and Nito's expenses at Grant Street. Dad figured maybe that was enough . . . if they all ate Cheerios and gnawed on chicken bones.

Mamita also hoped to get $1,000 from Switzerland

that could be converted to dollars by the Guaranty Trust of New York, then forwarded to a commercial account at the American Trust Company of San Francisco opened by my father.

Mamita was closing an account at Morgan & Company in New York and transferring the funds to Pop's regular Berkeley account.

My dad believed Mamita had ". . . income from a trust fund established, as far as I can see, in Kentucky. The money from this fund will (as plans now stand) be placed in a joint account of Monique and Mamita. I am in the process of investigating the practicality of this move."

Pop's letters to Grandpa asked, *What should I do?* He feared that Mamita's financial machinations would land him on Alcatraz in the middle of San Francisco Bay. Therefore, Grandpa should know that, "I am trying to send you a steady record of what is going on in certain branches of my life because I think there should be a record available somewhere in case the government (or anyone else, for that matter) takes a keen interest in the affairs of the people involved."

You would have thought he was laundering money, against his will, for what would be equal, in our modern times, to a Columbia drug cartel.

113.

Meanwhile, Monique was killing herself for Mamita and Ninon. Mamita preferred her meals to be formal, with candles, the proper place settings, the right kind of wine, and with doilies underneath the wine glasses. Think: "Merchant Ivory film." Everyone spoke French, that goes without saying. Perhaps Mamita could forgo the finger bowls, but not having a servant to dish up the evening meal was embarrassing.

One night, just to be funny, Monique and Ninon put on white blouses, a couple of Dad's ties, and dark blazers, and they painted on moustaches with eyeliner, or perhaps mascara, and served up the supper with mock formality to Nito and Mamita as the Brandenburg Concertos played softly on the background Victrola. The Robert sisters refused to sit down at the table, preferring instead to dine "with the help" in the kitchen. Mamita was a good sport, acting as if nothing were amiss. Nito gobbled his dinner too quickly, then excused himself to go study. Monique and Ninon could be heard laughing in the kitchen. Two prominent candles on the table burned softly to maintain the proper ambiance. Mamita did not abandon her dignity for a single moment. She rang the bell swiftly when her wine glass needed replenishment. And she rang it again—*ding*! *ding*!—when she was ready for her cheese, grapes, and a demitasse.

114.

My father rarely entered the house in time for dinner. I wonder why? If he did arrive *à table*, Mamita pointedly corrected his French whenever he butchered the pronunciation or forgot to use the plural imperfect subjunctive. Ninon giggled, enjoying his discomfort. Pop fumed silently. Monique spoke cheerfully and pretended nothing was wrong. One might think of her as an angel, seated on a puffy cloud, tapping the four cantankerous devils seated around her with a magic wand that transformed them into benevolent pals. My mom never tried to win you over with friendly persuasion. Monique simply projected her own sunshine that was totally free of antagonism. My dad put it this way: "She has an air of healthiness and good nature about her that no amount of fuss and dither can manage to dispel."

115.

Ninon kept bickering with my dad. She only used French with him, deliberately speaking too fast so that he had trouble understanding. They were born to snipe at each other. Why? I do know that Pop considered

Ninon sexy. She turned him on and was drop-dead gorgeous. Too, she had an edge and flustered him in an exciting way. The anger she triggered was erotic. Pop once told me that all men wanted to sleep with Ninon and I infer that included himself. Monique was not a vamp like her dark-haired sister, who, I believe, was attracted to my dad. This made for an emotional (a sexual) tension between Pop and Ninon to which Monique was oblivious. My dad also found Ninon to be spoiled rotten, featherbrained, vapid, imperious like her mother, and contemptibly vainglorious. In return, Ninon considered him an asshole and a loser, period. "*Tes oiseaux m'étouffent,*" she said. Your birds suffocate me. Left alone long enough they might have fucked each other.

116.

In Russia, Smolensk fell to the Germans, and the Third Reich's army surrounded Odessa. France's Vichy regime pledged itself to collaborate with the Nazi "New Order," and required all Jews in Paris to wear the star of David. Then they arrested five thousand Jews and sent them off to the Drancy concentration camp. German U-boats were sinking Allied ships plying the North Atlantic, and Winston Churchill and Franklin Roosevelt retaliated by signing the Atlantic Charter, promising

Monique and Ninon coming to America, 1936.

to destroy the Nazi and Vichy regimes. British and Soviet troops invaded Iran to push out the German aggressors. Kiev and Odessa continued holding up against the Third Reich's offensive. U.S. Secretary of State, Cordell Hull, warned the Japanese again not to mess with American shipping in the Pacific. And Hitler's troops next surrounded Leningrad, planning to starve the city to death with the help of that Spanish division. Franco might even send another division to aid the siege. Did that mean Spain would now officially join the Axis? If so, Mamita, Ninon, and Nito couldn't return to Barcelona. Which meant Ninon would be cut off from her current fiancé, Jorge Carreras Ribas, a member of Franco's Falange. They had plans for a Barcelona wedding in January.

Ninon grumbled hourly about "That stupid war in Europe." Why didn't America enter the war, bomb the Krauts, liberate France, and send Hitler packing? "You people are such *cowards.*"

I can't help but surmise that my father replied hotly in this vein: "It's not *our* war, we didn't *start* it, our leaders are *not* a gathering of fascist brutes, and it isn't our job to save you ninnies every time you decide to slaughter each other."

"Oh grow up," Ninon probably retorted in *this* vein: "Every time you open your mouth nothing but *merde* comes out."

Whereupon, Mamita most surely would have asked Nito to pour her another glass of Pouilly-Fuissé, and "pass the gravy boat, too, *s'il te plaît.*"

117.

On October 15, three weeks after Mamita and Ninon stepped off the train, my father muttered to Grandpa and Grammie that both he and Monique were pretty well pooped out. "Monique is very cheerful, but obviously very tired. Her hands have been bothering her, although they are improving under the constant care of skin specialist Dr. Allington. She has rather a mean pimple at the corner of her mouth, and has recently avoided having a vicious stye on her left eye by constant applications of hot water."

Too, the lines under Monique's eyes were getting deeper, and she had developed "a little stoop." My mom nervously snapped her nails together as she sat smoking for a few minutes after dinner. So Dad was planning to get her away from the house for a respite from family duties as soon as possible.

On that Friday, Monique met my father in San Francisco after his work. They had drinks at the Rainbow Room on top of the Mark Hopkins hotel, ate dinner in a Market Street bar & grill, then hopped a train to Salinas, a bus to Monterey, and a taxi to the Pine Inn at Carmel. Next morning, according to Dad in a letter to his parents, they were awakened at 6:30 a.m. by black phoebes. They breakfasted in front of a fire on waffles, eggs, sausages, bacon, jam and coffee, then walked to the beach where the surf was up and Heerman's gulls were playing surf-snipe, flapping clumsily aloft when overtaken by a wave. Scoters swimming along the breaker line dove under roiling whitecaps to avoid being smashed against the sand by the high surf.

My parents ambled along the beach hand in hand, watching birds. They felt momentarily back in their courting days at the William Floyd estate. A moment of reprieve. Pop described the scene: "It was one of those lead-gray semi-foggy days when everything looks closer or further and all sounds are slightly warped. One feels that one's dimensions have changed."

Later they headed into town, cruising the gift shops, buying nothing. After drinking hot chocolate at a Mexican café, they met friends who drove them to coastal hills overlooking the ocean for a picnic. "A black oystercatcher flew off squacking." Subsequently, they went to Point Lobos State Park and passed through a lovely cypress grove to a cliff rising above the ocean where black-vented shearwaters skimmed along the surface of the sea out from the shore. In the tide pools lived abalones. Lichen wisps dangled off cypress branches.

Come evening, "Monique got into a brand-new white blouse and yellow-corduroy-bell skirt, and I put on a very clean shirt and my pleasant-smelling and comfortable brown tweed suit. We descended to the ground floor and indulged ourselves in a glass of wine in the cocktail parlor of the hotel."

Surely that night they made love, very gently. Monique had been fragile ever since her "minor operation" in July. The stress of her family in residence was taking a toll but they didn't talk about that. Monique loved Mamita, Ninon, and Nito. She was very perceptive, yet had a remarkably loving tolerance of human personalities and foibles that intimidated my old man, and he did not know how to breach it. Under the covers in Carmel, Pop embraced my mom while she kissed him playfully, so grateful there would be no interruptions. She tickled him under the chin to make him smile, and teased him with loving expressions in French. When he talked back to her in French she corrected him the same as Mamita did at the dinner table until they were both giggling happily. They fell asleep with their arms around each other, and remained that way for many precious hours.

On Sunday morning they meandered along the beach again until chased away by a rain shower. After their final meal in Carmel, they caught the train back to San Francisco. Dad wrote: "As we pulled into the city a heavy rain storm was getting under way. There was no lightning, but the flashes of blue from the trolley-line joints and the red neon signs glistening on the wet rails and pavement gave that effect. There was no thunder, but fog horns and train whistles produced that effect. In searching my wallet I found that we had spent less than anticipated on the trip. So we had our last extravagance. We hired a taxi for $3.00 to take us back across the bay to 1710 Grant."

During the drive Monique rested her head in his lap. He placed one hand on her shoulder and sang softly, in French, the lullaby, *Fais Dodo*, with which Monique always laid me down to rest.

Go to sleep,
Monique, little sister;
Go to sleep
And you'll have a gift.
Momma is downstairs
Making chocolate;
Daddy is upstairs,
He's making a cake.
So go to sleep,
Monique, little sister;
Go to sleep
And you'll have a gift.

118.

Pop opened the commercial account for Mamita in his name at The American Trust Company, Market-Ferry office, San Francisco. Mamita suggested giving him power of attorney to conduct business on her behalf while she was absent from America. Then she discovered that her income would be taxed heavily if she wasn't living in the United States. Fortunately, Mamita's quota status gave her the rights of a resident. However, she and Ninon were now planning a return to Spain in December for Ninon's January wedding with Jorge Carreras. What if Mamita lost her U.S. resident privilege by leaving America? The French consulate in San Francisco determined that she could visit Spain for eight weeks without endangering her resident status. So Mamita decided to go but return promptly to Berkeley . . . much to my father's chagrin. He felt as if he'd become an indentured servant to Al Capone.

"P.S. Dear Dad," he moaned. "There seems to me to be much disagreeable, unpraisworthy money jealousy in the R. family at large. I have never yet let personalities influence my judgement. However, I am moved to rage and disgust by the ungrateful, egotistical, and thoroughly unsound way that Ninon looks at the family financial affairs—and this carries over to Mdme.

R. also at times. For Nito and for Monique I would do anything. They are wonderful. Nito's intelligence, gratitude, and thoughtfulness in all things would move anyone to love him."

119.

All this while it rained. It had been raining for days. Berkeley was drenched, drab, dull, soggy, depressing. At work, my dad observed that Japanese boats, which had been anchored in San Francisco harbor for months awaiting cargo, abruptly sailed off on November second, as empty as the brains of the idiots promoting warfare around the globe. *Now* what would happen? Was Pop about to be laid off? America and Japan were rattling more sabers at each other. Winston Churchill promised to join the United States "within the hour" if we declared war on Japan. Every morning, exactly at dawn, my father's eyes flew open and he was scared stiff about the day ahead. Monique and Johnny and the Barcelona contingent kept on sleeping as he listened to the bird songs beginning outside. He knew to which species each song belonged and that knowledge was soothing, it helped to calm him down. He remained uneasy, though, because clearly disaster and upheaval were all around us waiting to strike. Yet everybody was pretending that life goes on as usual, no big deal, what are we having for dinner? When Dad listened to his shortwave radio he felt clandestine, like a criminal, and kept the sound down low.

120.

But on November third, suddenly, a blessed reversal of fortune. Mamita and Ninon decided to leave for Barcelona on November 17. *Grâce à Dieu!* I don't think anyone asked outright for them to make tracks, yet they too must have been terribly uncomfortable. Fish out of water. In Spain there were *servants*. A cook, a maid, and the proper silverware and wine glasses. In Spain they would have a car and a chauffeur. In Spain no child could awaken them at two a.m. screeching from teething pains. In Spain, my father would not be a nervous wreck who callously ignored them by being at work in San Francisco all day long and then by doing his Russian translations at night at home instead of squiring them to restaurants and movies, or to concerts and upscale art galleries and museums across the bay.

And in an instant Mamita and Ninon were gone, off to Spain for Ninon's marriage to Jorge Carreras Ribas. What an incredible relief to Pop, probably also to Nito. I can't speak for Monique because nowhere (that I know of) did she bare her soul on the matter. However, although Ninon and Mamita had flown the coop, their melody lingered on. Almost as soon as his in-laws abandoned 1710 Grant Street, Dad was struck by a case of flu that knocked him for a loop and hijacked Monique and Nito along for the ride. No, they didn't catch the flu from him, but they experienced a very rough spell caring for my father, who plunged into despair during the illness. Wracked with fever, coughing up lungers, his head ached, his teeth ached, his back ached. He shivered all day and sweated all night, drenching the bed sheets. Wondering if he would die, he rued the muddle he'd made of life, essentially accomplishing nothing. He moaned and vomited, losing nine pounds in a week. He also came to the conclusion that Nito was a big intrusion on his privacy with Monique, his butterflies be damned. Increasingly, Monique's attention had been diverted from Dad by her family members and by me, and by her own freaky illnesses, her "ringworm" rashes, her disabled heart. A Greek chorus in Pop's brain persistently reminded him that these developments in his marriage had not at all been his intentions when he slipped an engagement ring onto Monique's finger and decided on "a course of action."

My mom listened to his protests without interrupting, and did what she could for her husband, rubbing his chest and shoulders with Vicks VapoRub and other cures of the day. He was grateful for the tea she made with lemon juice and honey. Only soft classical music issued from the radio. She read to him from a book in French and spread a cool washcloth across his brow. For long moments my mother sat beside the bed merely holding his hand, saying nothing while he attempted to sleep. When he had the strength to get up, she washed him gently in the bathtub. If possible, after the bath, she played guitar, singing him again to sleep with French lullabies and romantic ballads. But that didn't work much now. All the same, she was listening to his complaints with no attempt to defend herself. If I began to whimper in the background, it was Nito's job to quit studying and play with me or shove a bottle in my mouth. Nito always spoke French with me, and most often so did Monique.

121.

When Dad was awake, they talked. He poured out his laments and accusations, all the stress and anger and disappointment he'd repressed for ages. Apparently, he was coming unhinged again, same as at the start of this year when he'd fled back east in Martha Boyden's car. Monique listened with saintly patience. She would not remind him of how she had tried to break their engagement because she could foresee how difficult their marriage would be, and yet he had traveled to Paris and won her back anyway. She never would have said,

"I told you so." If now he didn't want to live with her anymore she would not plead her case, nor accuse him of prevarications and shortcomings himself. She would simply take Johnny and leave her husband in peace if that's what he wanted. Monique never proposed this vindictively. Her words were gentle, also sincere, and not phrased as a threat. They were *loving*. She loved him profoundly but understood in both her innocent and deeply wise way that you can't make another person love you if they don't wish to, and you mustn't attach yourself like a heavy rock to their ankles when they want or need to swim away.

A letter my dad sent to me in 1990 said this: "There was absolutely no question that Monique had a spiritual quality that quite a few people recognized. Monique also had an incredibly realistic streak. She was a child, but at the same time completely mature. It was an interesting combination. I once commented, 'I'm not good enough for you.' She told me, 'If you say that I might believe it.' She asked me, 'Do you like living with me? If you don't like living with me, I don't want to live with you.' She didn't mince words."

Almost twenty-five years earlier he had written these words in perhaps the first mention of my mother that he'd ever put down on paper for me: "Monique was a remarkable person . . . as you may have been told . . . different from Mamita like a Northwest clear-off [wind] differs from a Gulf Coast hurricane. She was one of the most forthright, unselfconscious, temperamentally balanced people I have ever known."

122.

Grammie and Grandpa scrutinized photographs of me that Monique sent to them. "Johnny is developing an interest in birds," she said, "and he likes to watch them come to the feeding-tray. He also has a passion for flowers and is always carrying one in his hand, whether a dandelion or something more fancy. He smells them deeply whether they have an odor or not, and even when it is only a picture."

As for my dad? Here was Monique's opinion: "Your son seems to have taken a definite turn for the better in his recovery from the flu. It certainly hit him hard, especially his spirits and, at one point, I almost thought he was on the verge of a nervous breakdown or something of the sort. But I think he has turned the corner now thank goodness. He is back at work regularly now."

123.

When he came up for air from his illness on December 6, Pop got in touch with Grandpa. "Back at work after a rather difficult relapse. My head is just beginning to clear. I came back to the office to keep from going batty, and I hope that this time I will be able to carry on without further setbacks."

That's a joke.

Next day the Japanese bombed Pearl Harbor.

124.

Quand il pleut, il pleut à verse. Bay Area air raid precautions became a hassle. Shops closed early and opened earlier. Train schedules changed. None of the American-Hawaiian ships were moving. Dad reported to his family back east, "Financial operations from Honolulu to mainland are temporarily out of whack. No cheques cleared from the islands and all the rest of it."

However, Pop conjectured that his present job might continue for at least six months. There seemed to be little chance that it would become advisable to move his family. Calls for civilian defense workers had been sent out. "Unfortunately, none of us is qualified for any of the work. My in-town activities, M's baby, and Nito's nationality seem to eliminate us from the field."

Regardless, the Pearl harbor attack had lambasted the American-Hawaiian Steamship Company and there were chances my father would soon be out of a job.

It was difficult not to feel doomed.

125.

Even Monique was stunned. For once her optimism took a holiday. America would no longer be a neutral refuge for her European friends and family members. And now all the Americans that she knew and loved, including her husband, could be drafted or put to work building weapons, or otherwise have their lives turned upside-down. About the war she herself declared it would "do no good to worry." How could a person change this irrevocable tide of hatred and devastation? My mom observed sadly, "The moon has certainly been beautiful of late." Yet because of air raid precautions and mandatory blackouts, "I suppose we must wish for less moonlight now."

126.

Grandpa opened letters from Pop dated December 20, December 22, two letters written on December 30, and another on the thirty-first. The main thrust of them was: "Help!" Typed at my father's San Francisco office, they were strained, frantic, paranoid, the world was caving in. Dad had applied to the Naval Intelligence Service for a position based on his skills with French and Russian. They gave him a rapid exam in French, and, ten days later, another examination in Russian. To my dad their attentions seemed half-baked, halfhearted, half insulting. Bureaucracy recapitulates stupidity. To be honest, his American-Hawaiian job was now up for grabs. The company's commercial relationships, so dependent on Japan, were nosediving toward oblivion. The old man had begun casting about for another job in case his current employment went south.

Across the bay, in Berkeley, Monique and Nito prepared for Christmas. There was a little tree, and beneath it the Woolworth's manger from last year with figurines from Germany, Italy, and England, and a few small black wooden animals making the crèche a cross between "the birth of Christ and Noah's Ark." Tiny birthday candles flanked the crèche. Monique sent out our Christmas cards—a blurry photograph of a dunlin in flight—and the greetings she and Pop received from friends were positioned on window sills and desk tops, the fireplace mantle, and the dining table. It was all very cozy and fun. She and my father slept downstairs now so that Monique could avoid going upstairs entirely.

Obviously, Christmas would not be as cheery this year as it had been before.

127.

David Nichols considered himself completely out of the holiday loop due to a lack of time and money. An expected bonus at the office had fallen through, what else would you expect? I have no letters from Monique to Grammie and Grandpa extolling the Christmas season. No doubt the war had put a serious damper on festivities.

Nevertheless, I cannot imagine my mother giving in to despair. Therefore, I envision her and Dad and Nito quietly observing the flickering candles beside their tree as they harmonized on "Silent Night" together. Monique held their hands. *"Douce nuit, sainte nuit, seule une étoile, dans le soir luit . . ."* My mom would have insisted on it. I would have been splayed out comfortably asleep on the rug at their feet sucking on my "blanky." And in their hearts, at least for the moment, there would have been peace.

128.

By the penultimate day of December, my folks were ill once more. Monique's hands exhibited the rash she had previously described as "ringworms." The eruptions did not respond to ointments or "ray therapy." My dad had another wicked cold. The Naval Intelligence Service concluded that Pop couldn't obtain a commission without a college degree. *Tant pis.* He felt it was beneath him to enter the service without a commission. That is, he wanted to be an officer. Really? Without a high school or college diploma he had about as much chance for a commission as a one-legged man in the proverbial ass-kicking contest.

129.

On New Year's Eve Nito was off skiing in the mountains, where, according to the news, major snowstorms raged. I have no description of how Pop, Monique, and yours truly celebrated the end of 1941. It can't have been very joyful. Yet my parents had many friends and I'll wager they got together at 1710 Grant Street that evening to celebrate with beer and wine and potluck dishes. They played records of the latest hit songs: "Pardon me boy, is that the Chattanooga Choo Choo?" Monique and Dad plucked their guitar strings as everyone sang boisterous versions of "Five Foot Two, Eyes of Blue," "Button up Your Overcoat," "I Want a Girl," and "Blue Moon." Many of the revelers liked to dance. It could be they listened to Dad's shortwave radio reporting on New Year's celebrations around the earth, in many languages, and despite the expanding world war. There were discussions about the latest Bay Area Christmas Bird Counts. They played charades, a game that Monique was good at: she could guess things instantly. My dad spoke Russian with a few of his "students" from the Museum of Vertebrate Zoology. They got a tad looped and began quoting Pushkin. Then Pop draped his arm over Monique's shoulders and together they recited perfectly, from start to finish, every verse of the Robert Service epic poem, "The Cremation of Sam McGee," which my dad had memorized in Cantwell, Alaska, while collecting small mammals for the American Museum of Natural History. After that they recited La Fontaine's fable, *The Crow and the Fox*, the first French poem my mom had taught to Dad.

Maître corbeau sur an arbre perché,
Tenait en son bec un fromage.
Maître Renard, par l'odeur alléché,
Lui tint à peu près ce langage . . .

They received a standing ovation!

130.

I'm not sure everyone stayed up until midnight. Most of them by now, like us, had kids, some of whom were sleeping on my parents' bed downstairs, Nito's bed upstairs, or on blankets off in a corner. But I would guess that at some point all the adults joined in to sing "Auld Lang Syne" with tears starting to well up because they understood their days together were ending, and nothing again would ever be the same. So *much* was ending. In the coming year their lives, their educations, their relationships would be irrevocably interrupted and changed forever by the war and most of them would be torn apart, drafted, shipped overseas, put to work in the war effort, flung to distant areas, and rarely, if ever, would any of them be brought back together again. Three years of academic and all-around general friendships and camaraderie were over. Finished. Kaput.

When people said goodbye at our door they embraced each other more warmly and longer than usual because they understood, instinctively, that they really *were* saying "Goodbye."

131.

Framing their rendition of "Auld Lang Syne" was a planet out of control, whirling toward an orgy of mass destruction. After Pearl Harbor, Japanese troops captured Wake Island; they were poised to take Manila; and Hong Kong and Malaysia would be next. Then Singapore. The United States had declared war on Japan, Germany, and Italy. Hitler, after suffering a bitter winter setback at Moscow, was cranking up his "final solution." Humanity had gone berserk.

And *everyone* wished for less moonlight now.

PART FIVE

Grandpa, Monique, and Bill Orton, Floyd estate, June 15, 1942.

132.

January 1942 was cold. As he walked to the Berkeley train station early one morning, Dad noticed ice on the puddles under fire hydrants. "This is unprecedented as far as my experience with this part of the world is concerned."

He shivered. Winter vegetables from their Grant Street garden froze. Monique wrapped herself in blankets. I lived inside my Dr. Dentons, and even wore a little sweater throughout the house and sometimes to bed. My mom had knitted a cap for me, but I yanked it repeatedly off my head. Don't fence me in!

Our family tried to be normal. On two different afternoons, in a borrowed car, Dad and Nito searched for clusters of migrating monarch butterflies roosting on Marin County eucalyptus trees. Nito was excited. He taped a skinny branch onto the handle of his butterfly net in order to reach up, capturing a few insects which he handled with great tenderness, reeducating Pop about their anatomy, their migration habits, their temperature controlling apparatus. You could tell a male by the black scent patches on its hind wings. Clearly, the monarchs were toxic with cardiac glycosides from feeding on milkweed plants and therefore quite unpalatable to birds. The current cold weather had bumped off many butterflies; their tattered wing bits lay on the ground like shredded leaves. Small predators, most likely mice, birds, possibly ants had eaten the bodies.

At the Museum of Vertebrate Zoology, Pop showed Nito (yet again) the mouse collections, explaining in detail, as he had on a few previous occasions, the variations of *Mus musculus*, its commensal and agrarian forms. The skull had sixteen teeth. He pointed out that the upper incisors were *not* grooved. They had ten mammae. House mice were very prolific, the females starting to breed at six to eight weeks and producing up to three litters of one to twelve offspring a year. Their lives lasted about five years. Their eyes could see for forty-five feet. The name *Mus musculus* derived from a Sanskrit word, *musha*, meaning "thief."

Nito, as always, was fascinated. By now he knew almost as much about house mice as Dad. Afterward, they drank beer at Spenger's Restaurant, talking nature with each other. Forgetting their limited capacities for booze, they each got tipsy on two beers apiece. And Nito relaxed enough to laugh out loud several times.

133.

On the whole, though, Pop was antsy and confused. If laid off by American-Hawaiian he might return to school for a spell. Frankly, that made no sense at all. It was difficult to figure out what *did* make sense.

My father considered quitting the steamship company and returning east to be closer to his family. The family he had fled because he'd wanted so badly to be *independent* after marrying Monique. That dream was a farce, wasn't it? Irony rules. He had made scant progress in education, nor could he earn a living that even partially supported his family. He continued begging on a regular basis for extra money from home. Push came to shove, there really was no escape from the trap he'd fabricated for himself, Monique, and me. Plans? What plans? When he'd arrived in Paris to win back the hand of his True Love, Mamita had pegged him immediately as a twenty-one-year-old indigent with no job, living on the family dole, absent any realistic prospects, and eager to impregnate her frail daughter prior to collapsing in a heap himself.

And look at him now. Mamita had had more prescience than a wizened gypsy with a crystal ball.

134.

Speaking of Mamita, she cabled that Ninon would marry Jorge Carreras in Barcelona on February 12, 1942. Then she hoped to catch a Clipper flight from Lisbon to New York. Mamita could not do the ticketing legwork from Barcelona. So would my dad please contact Pan American Airways on his mother-in-law's behalf and file an application for space on the Clipper plane from Portugal for her? Sure, why not? Pop had zero desire to host Mamita again, yet Mamita was Monique's mother so he kept his chickenshit mouth shut, and, like a good toady, hied himself to the offices of Pan Am and made the arrangements, seething with righteous indignation.

The world was at war. My old man could forget about salvaging his career because for the moment his career was in abeyance, irrelevant, over. And what *was* his career, anyway? Zoology? Political science? Slavic languages? Stevedore? Financial parasite? Mamita's eternal flunky?

135.

On January 20, 1942, Monique had a birthday party. Twenty-seven years old. Though my father told Grandpa there'd been a celebration, he gave few details.

A friend came over to the Grant Street house. They stayed up late. Maybe they played cards and sang songs: "Camptown Races," "*La Plume de Ma Tante*," "Home on the Range." Dad's letter to Grandpa was curt, it did not sound jolly. Party-goers must have been distracted by the war. Too much sorrow expanding around the globe. And America was in it at last. What else could a person think about?

I have no letters from Monique to Grammie and Grandpa about her birthday. No descriptions of her party. No descriptions of anything. Perhaps it felt almost like a crime to natter on about white-crowned sparrows, Nito's butterflies, and Johnny's charming flower sniffing while Americans were dying in the Philippines and so much misery existed elsewhere.

136.

The new year had arrived as a reinvented universe where catastrophe was breaking up "that old gang of mine." On the surface, things might look more or less the same, yet everything was different, cast in an alien light, and everybody had a new attitude framed by uncertainty because the security of our society was dissolving. All lives had been affected. Most plans—for jobs, education, family—were on hold or had already been altered or set aside. Abruptly our priorities were totally different or at least substantially undefined.

Dad ended a letter to Grandpa, saying, "Business is getting rocky. Don't know what's coming next."

Then he was laid off as private shipping came to a halt when the federal government took over *all* of American-Hawaiian's ships. The reverberations from Pearl Harbor had needed barely eight weeks to finish off our lives in Berkeley. I can't help but picture my father like a cartoon character, say Wile E. Coyote, out beyond the edge of a precipice spinning his legs frantically in the air trying to stay afloat just before plummeting two hundred feet onto a pile of rocks in the desert below.

137.

Pop's last letter dispatched from Berkeley to Grammie had this to say: "Plans are maturing rapidly. I am going to get away for the east as soon as possible. Probably within a week or so. If you have any extra money to give away for moving, it would be much appreciated at this stage in the game. I have just about enough to clear the trip, but I am not absolutely sure. Depends more or less on whether I can sell furniture to advantage. Nito will probably keep some if he takes room or apartment when we are gone. I have rough plans made for promoting my official status, they may or may not mature, but in any case I will feel a lot better to leave Nito on the West coast and get Monique off to myself for a while. I do not want her to get involved with her family in event I am drafted or otherwise removed from home."

Monique did not wish to leave Berkeley. She loved their house and their garden, and she had no desire to abandon Nito. They had grown close to each other in these past months. Nito was her one intimate blood connection to her family, to her culture and language, to her past history in another country on another continent, to her childhood and everything she loved and remembered about her former existence across the ocean. Nito was Monique's soulful bond to the whole other side of her heart.

My parents had a fight. Monique put her foot down. She loved her husband and had followed him faithfully and had worked on his behalf during every minute of their marriage, and she had listened to his complaints until the cows came home. That said, she also loved Berkeley and would *not* abandon her little brother, and my dad was a selfish man who rarely listened to anything Monique cared about, all he ever thought of was himself with no consideration for anyone else in the world aside *from* himself.

Dad slapped her, not hard, but he slapped her. Startled, Monique ran to their downstairs bedroom and locked the door, flinging herself onto the mattress, sobbing. Appalled by his own abrupt behavior, my father knocked on the door, he banged on the door apologizing through it. Monique refused to open up. She was terribly hurt and let loose a flurry of dismayed epithets in French that jolted her husband severely because she had never spoken to him with such alarming vehemence.

Pop lowered his shoulder and broke apart the flimsy latch. He grabbed my mother, weeping, and hugged her begging for her pardon, reproaching himself, and they held on tightly shuddering in each others' arms, both now repenting for their terrible behavior until they had calmed down and quit crying, and then they simply embraced until each in turn, exhausted, fell asleep.

Many decades later Dad told me, "That's the only fight we ever had."

138.

Mamita could not retain her seat on the Pan American Clipper. Instead, she sailed from Portugal on February 20, bound for New York. Ninon and her new husband, Jorge Carreras, stayed behind in Barcelona. As I vaguely remember the story, Mamita's ship required weeks to reach New York because it cruised down the west coast of Africa, crossed the South Atlantic to Argentina and proceeded north along the east side of South America, then snaked around the Gulf of Mexico along the shorelines of Venezuela, Columbia, and Panama and up the northern Gulf past Central America and Mexico, and then curved around to the Caribbean coast of Florida, and proceeded north again hugging Georgia, the Carolinas, and Virginia until at last it steamed past the Statue of Liberty into a berth at a west side Manhattan dock. Its roundabout route was intended to avoid the torpedoes of German submarines. Mamita may not have arrived at Peacock Point until late April or early May.

139.

Pop bailed. Monique and I traveled with him, leaving Nito behind in school to fend for himself. Years later my dad admitted that Monique had deplored the return east, she did not want to abandon Nito or their house in Berkeley. Too bad, you lose. My mother wept. Life was one damn upheaval after another. They sold most of the furniture, gave Nito a few pieces, and headed across country.

I guess what occurred next was inevitable, and it happened fast. We lived with Grammie and Grandpa for a spell at 116 Ninth Street in Garden City, close to New York. Maybe one week, perhaps two. Pop found another job, a temporary contract of six months with

Pan American Airways. He owed the employment to Bob Cummings, a stalwart at Pan American who had roomed with Dad's eldest brother, Floyd, at Harvard. Also instrumental was his childhood friend, Dorcas Oakley Ferris (nicknamed Dorcy), who was now married to Bob.

My parents located a modest apartment at 9 East 97th Street on Manhattan, close to Central Park. Grammie and Goggie Davison loaned us furniture and we moved in.

On May third Dad sent a grateful note to Grandpa at the American Museum: "Thanks very much for the May cheque, which came just in time to keep me out of jail."

140.

Surely we spent time with the Davison family at their New York apartments or out at Peacock Point. Goggie would have been so happy to see Monique again. And her daughter, Froggie Cheney, would have laughed and cracked a bunch of jokes and toasted my mom with champagne. Froggie and Monique were longtime good buddies and mischievous troublemakers at Peacock Point during their teenage years. Getting me baby sitters was as easy as saluting the flag, so Froggie and my mother attended a bunch of movies, like *My Gal Sal* with Rita Hayworth and Victor Mature; Jimmy Cagney in *Yankee Doodle Dandy*; and *Mrs. Miniver*, a film that featured Greer Garson and Walter Pidgeon. At Carnegie Hall they heard the New York Philharmonic, conducted by Serge Koussevitzky, play a program of Debussy and Tchaikovsky. And with Goggie along they even took in the Broadway revival of *Porgy and Bess*.

My dad was not much of a theater-, concert-, or moviegoer, so Monique was just catching up. Froggie and she drank more champagne and played Chinese Checkers and Monopoly in the breakfast nook at the Big House while being served deviled eggs and *petits fours*. Monique hadn't acted so free and silly in a while. At first she felt kind of awkward at Peacock Point. Then she played the piano and sang a duet with Froggie of "Summertime," from *Porgy and Bess*. They rehearsed it over and over again. They had all the words written on sheet music, and crooned repeatedly until their harmonizing was down pat. One of the butlers joined the song. A cocker spaniel galloped in barking and Froggie threw her shoe at it. Various children showed up from nowhere to listen. Even Goggie appeared in her dark, ankle-length dress and granny shoes with a loosely tied silk scarf around her neck, sitting on the couch with her arms around two little girls, so pleased to have my mother in the Big House again. Goggie's hat featured a bunch of fake plastic grapes on top cupped

Last picture of Johnny with Monique, June 15, 1942.

in a nest of cloth peony blossoms.

141.

At long last Mamita debarked in the United States where she hunkered down at Peacock Point or at Goggie Davison's East 67th Street apartment, and she and

Monique went off shopping at Abercrombie and Fitch, Macy's, and Bonwit Teller for blouses, skirts, slips, and chintz to cover a couch. Mom was overjoyed to see Mamita, whereas Pop maintained his distance as much as possible. He honestly couldn't believe that his mother-in-law was back in the mix again. Well, whatever. When Dad wasn't at the office he continued his Russian translating at home before bed. Monique, exclusively, watched after me. Approaching my Terrible Twos I was a bloody handful, running her ragged with more noisy energy than a fire engine racing toward a five-alarm blaze.

"I just want to feed him a great big meal and then go to sleep for twenty-four hours," she moaned. "*Je dormirai comme une marmotte.*"

"Let's put some phenobarbitol in his pablum," Froggie suggested.

142.

I have three pictures of my family that are all dated June 15, 1942. Taken on the front lawn of the William Floyd estate at Mastic, they include me, Grandpa, Monique, my dad, and his friend Bill Orton, an airplane pilot for BOAC whose American terminal was located in Baltimore. That lovely expansive lawn was almost as long and wide as a football field. These are the last photographs of Monique that I have in my possession.

First composition:

My grandfather, John T. Nichols, a pipe clamped between his teeth and formally attired in his rumpled blue serge Brooks Brother suit and tie, heads toward the left frame. Monique stands midphoto, hands raised behind her head rearranging her hair band or a barrette. She faces right, talking to Bill Orton, who is gripping what seems to be an 8 millimeter movie camera. Monique wears a white jumper over a blouse with the sleeves rolled up. Bill wears a short-sleeved white shirt and pleated trousers. It is a sunny day around noontime judging from Bill's shadow. The lawn stretches away behind Grandpa, Monique, and Bill to a line of trees along the sandy Indian Point road. Situated a couple of hundred yards into those trees is the Floyd family cemetery.

Some months later Bill Orton would be shot down and killed over Norway while flying war materials for the Brits.

Second composition:

My skinny dad, 25, lounges on the front lawn showing me an object we're both intently inspecting.

What is it—a tobacco pouch? I can't tell. Nearby, Bill Orton lies stomach down on the grass raised slightly on his palms, peering over at Dad and me. I intuit we are playing a game. Monique is out of frame, not visible.

Third composition:

Monique, on the front lawn of the old William Floyd house, hands on her hips, glances down at yours truly who is tugging at her skirt, my head tilted back looking up, and, obviously, I am imploring my mom for something. Probably attention. Monique is laughing. I am almost twenty-two months old. Behind us is the Floyd house, a white wooden structure of two floors with a shingled roof. You can see half the screened front porch, the ground-floor windows of the main house's old dining room, three upstairs windows of the main hallway and the Rose Bedroom. The entire east wing is visible, too, three windows on both floors. Dark shutters flank each window, shutters behind which bats sleep during the day. I know this fact because a few years hence, whenever my family visited Mastic, the first thing we would do was look for sleeping little brown (*myotis*) bats behind those shutters.

This is the last picture of Monique alive. The last picture of me with my mom.

143.

Abruptly, Pan American transferred my father from his New York office to their Miami headquarters. So he hit the road again in late June, 1942, leaving Monique and me behind until he could manage to rent a home for us down south.

Before he left, Dad helped Monique close down our Manhattan apartment: family members lent helping hands. Monique and I lived for a spell in Garden City with Grammie and Grandpa. In Miami, after work and on weekends, Pop searched for a place to rent. He found a Coconut Grove cottage but couldn't move in because there was no furniture, no ice box, no stove. The furniture would be shipped down from up North. It had been loaned to us by Grammie and Goggie Davison.

Meanwhile, my dad bunked at a comfortable Miami Beach home owned (or perhaps rented) by Bob and Dorcy Cummings. Monique and I squatted with Grammie and Grandpa for a short spell, then we switched to Mamita at Peacock Point. Monique was "involved again with her family" while Dad "was removed from home." Not for long, though. In early July, after getting a high sign from Miami, my mother and I kissed Mamita goodbye at New York's Pennsylvania Station and climbed aboard the Tamiami Champion train to Florida.

For the record: The Japanese had taken Singapore and the Philippines and initiated the Death March of Bataan. Then they bombed Port Darwin, Australia, invaded New Guinea, and captured Java. German and Italian troops occupied Benghazi. The Nazis continued their Final Solution, sending Jews to Auschwitz while overrunning Sebastopol. You could not begin to describe the Russian carnage from Stalingrad through Moscow to Leningrad. The United States felt compelled to intern 100,000 Japanese-Americans at home while fighting the naval battles of Midway and the Coral Sea abroad. The British were attacking El Alamein. And U.S. bombers made mincemeat of Rumanian oil fields at Ploesti.

144.

Monique and I arrived in Miami Beach on July 8, and we moved in with Bob and Dorcy Cummings. I have four letters that were written by Monique, dated July 6 through July 16, 1942. They are in French and addressed to Mamita. The letters were discovered by my first cousin, Véronique Robert, in the basement of her parents' Alicante (Spain) home after her father died, and she sent them to me. Véronique's father was my Uncle Nito. He succumbed to Alzheimer's at age seventy in 1995.

The four letters from Monique are gentle and chatty, very calm. The train trip was great. "Johnny was well-behaved and had a lot of fun. Dave met us at the station looking very handsome in a light gray suit, and you can imagine how happy we were to be together again."

Dad drove us in a rented car over to Coconut Grove to see our new house. Monique thought it was perfect. She described it as having a "big living room, two small bedrooms, a miniscule dining room, kitchen, bathrooms, and many cupboards. In front there's a sort of drive in a half circle with lawns and bushes fronting other houses. To the left in back there's a little garden with a lawn protected and shaded by a high wall, and circled by fences on other sides making it a dream place for Johnny."

Miami was very hot. You sweated from morning to evening. The nights were cool, happily. "The first night was not so great because my poor little sonny-boy had a terrible teething attack plus the heat. I spent the entire night getting him back to sleep and catnapping when I could."

Though happy to be at Bob and Dorcy's place, she yearned to fix up the cottage. "Dave is hoping that our furniture will arrive next week. I'm so impatient to be in our own house and to fix it up. Dave works a lot

194

and seems happy. We are so delighted to be together again."

But she didn't regret at all staying behind and having such a good time with her mom.

145.

Monique's fourth letter, mailed from Miami Beach on July 16, is also matter-of-fact. Johnny had gotten over his cold. She could write just now because I was conked out for the moment. Her family is happy and relaxed. She's excited because the furniture is supposed to arrive today and then they'll be able to take possession of their new home in Coconut Grove. Monique is getting used to the climate. She's starting to tan pretty good, and cut an inch and a half off her hair due to the heat. Next time she gets a permanent she might try something a bit fluffier. Yesterday she went swimming with friends in a borrowed suit, but the water was really *hot*. She had fun anyway. My parents have caught lots of butterflies that Monique will send to her brother Nito in Berkeley tomorrow.

"I think he'll be happy because there are many different kinds and they are beautiful."

So life was lovely and fun. And the most fun happened a couple of days ago when Monique and Pop hired a babysitter and went out for a night on the town.

For me, these are Monique's last words.

146.

"I wore my dress with red and white piping and shoes to match. It was marvelous. And I was so happy to wear little panties to match because a slip would have been too hot. Dave really admired my outfit, he was excited to see me looking so chic. First we went to dinner at the Chicken Coop here in Miami Beach, a precious place right on the water. Then we crossed the bay to Miami. There, we had a drink at the Shell Bar of the Colonial Hotel. Everywhere, you could only see officers of the army and the navy, soldiers and sailors. It was nevertheless really cheerful and fun. Then we went to the Clover Club where people can dance and we danced. Finally, we went to the Club Bali, a cool place that is really friendly and cheerful. It was full of officers from the Dutch and Norwegian navies. We stayed to watch the floor show, then we danced until after midnight. In summation, it was a terrific evening and my dress was a *fabulous* success."

PART SIX

Johnny in Miami Beach, August 4, 1942.

147.

Four days later my mother entered St. Francis Hospital in Miami Beach. July 21, 1942. Two days before my second birthday. That was the day, according to my father, that I supposedly put together my first complete French sentence: *"Maman fait dodo."* Mommy is taking a nap. Monique and I had been in our new home town for only thirteen days. The furniture for our rental cottage had arrived on July 16. Movers unloaded it at the Coconut Grove place. My parents took possession of that house a day later and began arranging things. They purchased an ice box and installed it in the kitchen. For four days, while Dad went to work, my mom cared for me and unpacked dishes and silverware and clothes. Maybe she put up curtains. Did she wear white cotton gloves for the "ringworm" eczema on her hands? What truly *was* that problem anyway?

I wonder if Monique was pushing around furniture when she became ill. How did the staph infection begin inside her heart? And when? Could it have been simmering for a while? An infectious endocarditis staph infection, according to my *Merck Manual*, is similar to a strep infection ". . . but the course is more rapid. ABE can develop on normal valves and is marked by the variable presence of high fever, toxic appearance, rapid valvular destruction, valve ring abscesses, septic emboli, an obvious source of infection, and septic shock." The *Manual* adds: "Without treatment, IE is always fatal."

148.

An ambulance carried Monique from Coconut Grove to St. Francis Hospital. This I note from reading a list of medical expenses my dad drew up at the end of her first week at the hospital. St. Francis was located on Allison Island near the start of North Beach, in the middle of Indian Creek, right where the 63rd Street bridge over Indian Creek connected to Collins Avenue which ran on a narrow strip of land beside the Atlantic Ocean.

The hospital has since been demolished. It was a bright white edifice that, according to one Internet user with a long memory, "looked more like a country club than a hospital." It stood at the southern tip of narrow Allison Island and was surrounded by palm trees and water.

Knowing Monique, she may have written a few more letters while hospitalized. A year before he died, my dad conjectured, "Possibly Grammie threw out letters which Monique wrote while in the hospital . . . and/or other letters by friends, helpers and family." He was able to locate none of those letters in his extensive files.

149.

Monique submitted to multiple blood transfusions and X-rays. Her spinal fluid was tapped, oxygen was administered, she had electrocardiograms. Oddly, her doctor's name was Dr. Nichol.

My father visited every day, and he also went to the Pan Am office. He needed his salary and could not quit the job. As new arrivals in Florida, Monique and David had few friends except for Bob and Dorcy Cummings. Who else from the Miami area, if anyone, visited the hospital while Monique was there? My father never said because I don't believe I ever asked him that specific question.

He hired a nanny to look after me.

150.

No doubt Monique slept most of the time. What thoughts might she have had? Was she afraid? What sort of conversations were shared with Dad? How long could he stay during visits? Would he stand at the window reporting on bird life in the palm trees, or on the canal? Did my mother speak much with the nurses? Were her doctors forthcoming? Did they explain the situation? Was there access to a telephone? Did Monique converse by phone with Mamita during those days? Had Mamita been informed of the true nature of her daughter's serious illness? Perhaps Dad told Mamita to stay out of it the same way he had ordered Grammie to keep her opinions to herself about Monique's "very minor operation" in Berkeley.

I don't think you should approach the dangerous province of giving medical advice about my family.

151.

Most of what I know about my mother's first week in hospital derives from Dad's panic, in his letters, over the costs of her illness. After making a list of expenses, he began pleading with friends and family for aid. The hospital room cost $8.00 per day. A portable chest X-ray had cost $15.00. Special nurses were $24.50. Laboratory fees had come to $74.00. Drugs to $19.64. Kleenex was $.90. Telephone calls to New York and Portland, Oregon, $16.35. Oxygen, $38.00. Transfusion, $5.00. Electrocardiogram, $10.00. Ambulance, $5.00. Saline solution, $15.00. The big gun, a staph antitoxin, had cost $132.00. The nurse who cared for Monique during the day charged eight bucks per shift. Same price for the nurse who attended my mother after dark.

When Pop toted up these charges they came to $653.39. The phone call to Portland, Oregon, was to request a dose, or doses, of penicillin. The antibiotic had been made effective against certain bacterial infections by British scientists in 1941. In March of 1942, the first American civilian to be saved by penicillin was Ann Miller of New Haven, Connecticut. Yet half the total available supply of the drug had been needed to treat her. By June, 1942, there were only enough effective stocks in the country for ten patients, and those units were destined for military use overseas. Goggie Davison pulled every string she could to have a small amount of the "wonder drug" flown across country from Oregon for Monique, but she did not succeed. Come February 1943 enough penicillin had been synthesized to treat one hundred patients. Ironically, later in 1943 over two hundred million units of the antibiotic were produced, almost all of them sent to our armed forces at war. Penicillin was made available to the U.S. general public on March 15, 1945.

152.

Grandpa hired a New York cardiologist, Harold Pardee, who caught an emergency flight to Miami and consulted on Monique's case. He thought she would be okay and charged $1,200.00 for his opinion.

Pop sent a letter to Grandpa on July 29. It was an itemized account of the first week's expenses, exclusive of doctor's services. He estimated that he would need a minimum of twenty-five hundred dollars more in addition to all that had been made available to date. He was writing to Goggie Davison with a copy of the account and would be gratified if Grandpa would speak to her, to Uncle George, and to Uncle William concerning finances. However, it was pretty hard for him to see just where, how, and when the money for this problem could be raised.

"If I am unable to obtain enough money from family sources," my dad said, "I will run up some debts here in Miami."

On that same day he addressed Goggie, thanking her for her check of one thousand dollars. He attached another account of his first week's expenses and said, "I would be very pleased if you would talk over the financial situation of this problem with my mother." He was terribly grateful for her contributions.

153.

On August first Pop told Grandpa:

"A large number of the staff of our offices have contributed blood for Monique. This has very materially decreased my expenses and very materially increased my morale. I have received notification of deposit of fifteen hundred dollars, ($1,500.00) to my account by Uncle William [Grandpa's brother]. Attached is a brief account of other expenses paid to date and subsequent to the account of July 28." [They added up to $557.00.]

Dr. Nichol had been pessimistic last night. Dad hadn't yet received this morning's report. Things were going along about the same. He would notify Grandpa immediately of "any marked change one way or another."

154.

Perhaps Monique and David talked about camping in Nevada, or inspecting *Mus musculus* specimens at the Los Angeles museum, or how difficult it had been to make love without waking Johnny up. But I know that's just romantic twaddle, movie stuff. In these situations most communication, if any, is at a morose and monosyllabic level. The woman felt miserable and was fighting for her life. Seated and leaning forward with his elbows on his knees, Dad stared at his exhausted wife sucking oxygen . . . from a mask? From a tube in her nose? It's sad no other family members were on hand to support him. To support her.

Decades later Pop recalled for me that when a doctor near Monique's bed suggested there was little hope, she heard him and opened her eyes, saying, "I don't want to die."

155.

Tonight, right this minute, I am a 77-year-old man picturing my 27-year-old mother asleep at St. Francis Hospital of Miami Beach seventy-five years ago. A nurse takes her pulse and leaves quietly. I think of Dad carrying Monique up the stairs at 1710 Grant Street. I see them holding hands at the railroad station in Paris when he arrived to mend their broken engagement. Side by side, crouched in a bird blind, they peep out at wandering tattlers on the beach. They kiss each other trapped in their own kitchen closet at 1713 Dwight Way. An elderly hitchhiker plays the "Marseillaise" on his violin for Monique as the Grease Pig cruises toward Nevada. And, both my parents peering through binoculars, they count waterbirds at Berkeley's Aquatic Park.

Almost exactly one year earlier my father had written this to Grammie describing his Berkeley life with Nito and Monique:

"No words can describe the intense excitement, the wonder, the prayers, the longings, the flashes of devotion, friendship, disgust, reluctance, dismay, and determination which are exchanged between the three of us every day. Here is a household of cultured, sensitive, widely experienced young people working at their problems together—not always in harmony— always with faith in themselves. To decide that this or that will be done with Nito is far beyond the reach of cold intellect. We'll just take it easy—do the best we can—not tire ourselves out by swimming against the undertow—and adjust the details as they come up. I doubt that any of us would care to part company— more especially in difficult times."

Now, many details were being adjusted and they had parted company in difficult times. Most likely Dad stood by Monique's hospital window gazing out at birds preening among the palm branches or hovering to snatch mosquitoes from the air. Would pelicans have flown by? Taking a break while Monique slumbered, he may have walked over to the Atlantic Ocean beyond Collins Avenue where sandpipers scampered along the wave lines playing surf-snipe.

And my father may have wondered if Nito had yet

received the butterflies he and Monique mailed from Miami to Berkeley on July 17th, barely over a week ago.

156.

According to her death certificate, my mom died at 12:30 p.m. on August 4, 1942. Shortly after lunch, I suppose, although Dad told me she had died at night. 12:30 a.m.? Perhaps the death certificate was typed incorrectly.

In any case, neither my father nor Mamita were there. None of Monique's family were present. She died alone. A doctor, not Dr. Nicol, but rather Guy Stoddard, signed the death certificate. The cause of death? "Acute bacterial endocarditis due to Staphylococcic septicemia due to rheumatic heart disease." My mother had been hospitalized fourteen days. The person who supplied information for her death certificate was Bob Cummings—Robert L. Cummings, Jr., my father's colleague at Pan American.

Removed from hospital to the Niceley Funeral Home of Miami Beach, Monique's body was drained of blood so she could be embalmed. Although he was telephoned immediately at work, my father never saw her body. I wonder if anybody had taken me to visit her at St. Francis Hospital, or were little kids not allowed? I presume the latter. My mom departed from

208

my life when she left our new Coconut Grove cottage by ambulance on July 21, 1942, two days before my second birthday.

I never said "Goodbye," only *"Maman fait dodo."*

157.

Pop phoned Grammie and Grandpa, and then he may have mustered all his strength to ring Mamita at Peacock Point. Or perhaps he left the job to his parents. That makes more sense. Mamita immediately flew to Miami where I gather she took care of the mortuary details. To me, many decades after the fact, Dad was emphatic that Mamita did *not* come to Miami until *after* Monique was dead. She would have wanted to see the corpse before it was sealed in a coffin. I don't know why I assume that, just instincts. Afterward, the screws were tightened down and they may be like that today. In 2017 does anything remain of Monique's coffin buried at the William Floyd estate?

When I asked my dad for his recollections of the period following her death, he could hardly remember. According to his financial accounts, the Niceley Funeral Home charged $495.00 for their services. The Atlantic Coast Line Railroad that carried Monique's body to New York billed him $246.18. Pop took leave of his job with Pan American Airways for a few days, but only a few days. He and Mamita flew north. I remained behind in Miami Beach.

My mother's body went by train to the William Floyd estate at Mastic. Although Monique was Catholic, the priest from Center Moriches, the town next door to Mastic, refused to say funeral mass because the rest of our family was Protestant. Grandpa knew a fellow from the Catholic hierarchy who convinced a New York priest to officiate. "He did an excellent job," Pop related two years before *he* died. "He saw immediately that there were a wide range of family connections and emotions. He had to be conciliatory, and he was."

158.

Monique was buried at the Floyd estate in the middle of summer, between August 6 and August 9. I can't know for certain who, besides Grammie and Grandpa, my dad, and Mamita attended the funeral. I'm sure that Goggie Davison motored over from Peacock Point with her son Trubee, daughter Froggie Cheney, and others from the Davison family, they all loved my mother. I'll wager that even the butlers, Bedford and Frederick, came. I know Dad's sister Mollie Weld attended despite having three small kids to care for. My father's brothers, John and Floyd, may have been present, Floyd with Catherine, his fiancée. I wonder if

John and Floyd had joined the military yet?

On which day, exactly, was she buried? Nobody signed the Floyd house guest book during the week after August fourth. Dad once said that funeral services at the estate were held indoors, in the front parlor and hallway. Traditionally, they conducted no ceremony at the graveyard. What did everyone do, then, after the indoors service, simply stand quietly in the cemetery while the coffin was lowered and somebody filled in the hole? Or was that an indelicate task performed out of sight by gravediggers? My father never described for me any of the details.

Let's say a smattering of mourners watched Monique return to earth. August at the William Floyd estate can be uncomfortable because of heat and humidity, mosquitoes, and many ticks. There would have been plentiful birds, catbirds and robins, towhees, vireos, ovenbirds, and blue jays. From my childhood summers I remember brown skipper butterflies at the honeysuckle vines attached to white latticework around the eastern door of the old house. I recall rabbits on the front lawn and whip-poor-wills come evening.

It's a small, grassy cemetery surrounded by a simple white wooden fence. A couple of pine trees and a few bushes stand among the graves. There are about sixty markers in it today; I don't know how many were there in 1942. Some stones date back to the late 1700s. In advanced age William Floyd moved to upstate New York and died there, but his original gravestone was later transferred back to Mastic. It lies flat at the back of the plot.

Outside the graveyard proper are a half-dozen white wooden crosses, on them the first names of slaves who died while working at the estate.

159.

I suspect the Nichols remained stoic New Englanders throughout my mother's funeral service. Mamita sobbed. The Davisons and their ilk must have borne up much like Grammie and Grandpa, except for Froggie Cheney who wept uncontrollably throughout. By and large, emotional excess was considered unseemly by their caste of moneyed aristocracy. Perhaps my father cried, although I would guess he labored to fulfill his mother's wishes by keeping stern and in control. Undoubtedly, he was in shock. If he now shed tears at Mastic, they were released in private. It certainly would not have been appropriate to "go off the deep end." Grammie would not have approved, would she? Just suck it up. Puritans don't cry.

160.

However, they *are* prone to fear and guilt. And Mamita had already put the arm on Dad concerning my future. She wanted me raised French, preferably in Europe, or, if in America, by herself with the collusion of Goggie Davison and the human and economic infrastructure at Peacock Point. Their contentious vying for legal custody of me had begun and Pop was most likely preoccupied by preparing himself to go to war with his mother-in-law. In 1942 *women* raised the children. Period. As a single man, Pop did not have a chance of retaining legal control of me. That said, not until hell froze over would this imperious and manipulative French hoity-toit wrest possession of his son from David Nichols.

But he was scared. Mamita had Goggie and the Davisons on her side. And the Davisons were powerful. They possessed plenty of money for lawyers, judges, social workers, nurses, doctors, nannies, French tutors, food, clothing, toys, and a topflight private education for Johnny. They were beacons of security and stability who could fork over the passage on ocean liners that would carry me to Mamita's house in Barcelona. Then Mamita would take me to Paris and out to the family homeland in Brittany . . .

161.

Dad knew the cards were stacked against him. And already, before the first serious confrontation with Mamita, he felt at a big disadvantage. For starters, he was riven by guilt. Probably he didn't *deserve* to own me. How come he'd not seen Monique's death coming and therefore adjusted their lives accordingly? All the signs had been obvious. He had not taken her heart problems seriously enough. Why did he move us to a two-story house on Grant Street where my mom had to climb the stairs? What was he *thinking*? How could a person be so self-centered and oblivious? Her "very minor operation" had emphasized my mom's vulnerability, and yet. And yet then he allowed Mamita and Ninon, during their 1941 visit, to drive his wife like their Cinderella slave while he mostly avoided home and rarely pitched in.

By what right had he forced her to marry him in the first place? Talk about hubris and blind ego. How could he steal her from her family and from her country when it was on the verge of a war? Next, though he understood she was frail, he impregnated her with a child that almost killed her, and whom he could not financially support. Long after Dad's passing I read some journals he kept during the early 1970s. On

March 7, 1971, he wrote: "Raise the point, here, that Mamita was opposed to our marriage, and that I felt guilty and somehow responsible for Monique's death."

His journal for January 16, 1972, said: "In writing this down I recall flying to Mastic with Mamita for Monique's funeral . . . the people milling about the hall . . . Mamita may have felt that I was responsible for Monique's death. I wonder if Dad did?"

Another long and pretty frantic journal entry asked the same questions on June 28, 1971. Pop recalled my birth at Alta Bates Hospital in Berkeley, Grammie's presence at the hospital, his own nervousness, his fear of having a child, and Monique's pain as a result. In the middle of free associating from a dream, he had a ". . . sudden concern to talk the whole thing over with [his Denver psychiatrist] Graham . . . does my analysis neurosis clustering indicate I am responsible for something? Responsible for making unwanted child with Monique . . . responsible for hurting her . . . killing her? I did not meet my responsibilities with Monique . . . fiscal . . . connubial . . . forcing the marriage was taking too much responsibility . . . I had no right to have children in the first place . . ."

And here's the last paragraph of a letter he wrote me a few years before his death:

"I was not a good husband to her. I loved her dearly and never overcame the loss. One of the reasons I did not overcome the loss was because, deep down, I recognized that I had not given her even a smitch of what she gave me. I was unable to let myself go, give up my own narcissistic drives and needs even for short spells, in order to render her unconditional love."

162.

I have a series of three black and white photographs taken in Miami or Miami Beach while Monique was hospitalized or immediately after she died. I intuit that the pictures were made on the day of her death. Those three images focus on a circular basin, about eight feet across, full of water that is partially covered by lily pads. The rim around the basin is a foot wide, tiled, and with four circular clay pots arranged equidistant on the tile rim. The water is perhaps a foot and a half deep. At the center of the basin, on a pedestal, stands a small naked cherub holding up a hose.

In one photo I am alone, leaning over the rim splashing my hands in the water. I'm not wearing a shirt. I have just turned two years old.

In the next picture I am still alone, though seen from a different angle. An archway behind me has a terra-cotta roof. It is typical Florida architecture.

The third image records me standing at the basin's rim staring upwards at a water jet rising from the cherub's hose. Two men and two women are in the photograph. I recognize none of them. The picture is blurry. The lady standing directly behind me wears a shirtwaist dress. I sense that this could be the nanny Pop hired to care for me while Monique was hospitalized. Another woman in a lightweight summer dress squats to the left of me beside the basin. Her knees are exposed. She is looking over at me. I cannot make out her features, yet something about the hairstyle is vaguely familiar, as if she might be family. But who? The two men stand behind us on the right side of the photograph. One, a thin guy in a tan army uniform, is adjusting his tie. The other man, sporting a light-colored Palm Beach suit and dark tie, stands with hands on his hips. Although he seems familiar, I cannot place him. Could he be my Uncle John, Pop's brother, the middle Nichols boy? Or is he my father? The two men look over at me gazing up at the water jet rising from the cherub's hose. Obviously, I am awed.

I know that all three snapshots were taken in Miami or Miami Beach the first week of August 1942. Again, I feel strongly they were made either while my mom lay dying, or on the day of her death. To me the photos are pulsating with Monique's intimate presence and with her mortality. So even today, at age seventy-nine, these blurry pictures make me feel a palpable sorrow at losing what might have been.

AFTERMATH

Monique in Arizona, age 18, February 1933.

163.

In 1986 Pop retired from a successful career teaching psychology for twenty years at the University of Colorado in Colorado Springs. He and his fourth wife, Jackie Newberry, moved to a small town called Smithville near Austin, Texas, and, at age eighty-one, my father died there of prostate cancer on April 13, 1998. We were close, and I loved him dearly.

Two years after his passing I flew to Texas, got a U-Haul truck, and brought Dad's massive archives north to my hometown of Taos, New Mexico, where I rented a storage locker solely to house those archives. I was sixty years old. Over the next three years I methodically read through the old man's files and Xeroxed any materials connected to Monique. I was seeing most of them for the very first time. Then I shipped untold boxes of the archives to my half-brother Dave in Mt. Kisco, New York, where he stored them in his garage and attic. Dave was seven years younger than me.

While slogging through thousands of file folders I found many letters written by Monique, and much correspondence between Dad and Grammie and Grandpa when he and Monique were married and even during the two weeks she lay dying in Miami Beach. As I worked through the archives I also began at last to read a couple of Monique's teenage diaries that I obtained late in my own life but had largely ignored.

One of those diaries describes her second visit to America. She arrived, accompanied by Auntie May, the autumn of 1932. And when reading her journal entry for Christmas Eve at Peacock Point that year I came upon her remark that Trubee Davison was filming Goggie as she read *The Night Before Christmas* to a group of children and grownups waiting to hang up their stockings at a large fireplace in the Big House.

Immediately, I wondered if any of the Davisons had saved those 8 millimeter movies or perhaps had them transferred to a videotape.

So I wrote to Danny Davison.

Danny (the son of Trubee Davison) and I had been exchanging Christmas greetings for years. After Goggie, and then Froggie Cheney, died, Danny was my main connection to the Davison family, also my benefactor (and legal representative) in America when Mamita passed away. A banker at J.P. Morgan for much of his career, Danny then headed the United States Trust Company for over a decade until he retired at sixty-five. He had a great sense of humor and often reminded me that he looked forward eagerly to my Marxist-Leninist Christmas letters. Danny died in 2011, eight years before I completed this story. That makes me sad.

164.

A month after I approached Danny about those 8 millimeter films, a package arrived from Peacock Point. It contained a VHS tape that had compilations of several old Davison home movies. Some had been filmed from an airplane during an African safari. Others captured the iconic aviator, Charles Lindbergh, at Peacock Point one Fourth of July floating helium balloons into the sky for kids to shoot at with Roman candles. And, incredibly, there were scenes of Goggie at Peacock Point reading to children and adults gathered before her on Christmas Eve, 1932.

I held my breath, wondering if Monique would appear.

And, yes, she is there listening to Goggie along with the other children. The little girls have bows in their hair and for the most part are wearing white chiffon dresses. A small cute boy has on a sailor blouse. Nito's future wife, Diane Gates, has blond hair and looks to be about six. She is the adopted child of Alice Gates, Goggie and Harry Davison's eldest daughter. I think I can identify Danny Davison also, who must be seven or eight.

Monique will soon celebrate her eighteenth birthday. She is wearing a simple, long-sleeved jersey with the hem around her hips. At her waist is a narrow belt. Her hair is cut really short so it goes only halfway down her neck, but it also covers her ears and comes out into a curl against the back of each cheek. Froggie Cheney is among the nearby adults, acting irreverent, and she has the same haircut as Monique. It must be the style of that day. At one moment Froggie holds a scarf mockingly over her face. Monique keeps her arm protectively around a little girl, and turns toward the camera twice when saying something cheerful to the child. My future mother's eyes sparkle, her smile is shiny, her cheeks glisten, her teeth are perfect and very white. The camera pans, so it holds on Monique for only a few seconds, yet she is attractive, vibrant, *gleaming.*

Then one by one, helped by grownups, the kids march up to pin their stockings on a line extending to either side of the fireplace mantle. Monique also clips on her stocking, apparently the only "grownup" doing so. When finished, she turns to go out of frame and her dazzling smile is for a second aimed toward the camera. She stops my heart. How stunning it is for me to see her "alive!"

I was sixty-two years old when that VHS tape arrived

at the Taos post office six decades after Monique's death. The filming had been done almost nine years before I was born.

165.

In a letter dated January 26, 2000, my friend Danny Davison remembered Monique clearly although he had been only seven or eight when my mother first showed up at Peacock Point in 1931. He said:

"I do remember your mother. She was an elderly woman, probably in her late teens. She was a pied piper and had a corps of apostles following her, hanging on every word which as I recall were numerous. She looked more like you than anyone else in the family—handsome rather than beautiful. Monique seemed to be interested in everything. I remember a gay bubbly person with laughter and smiles all around. She was also kind. I remember her returning from a trip out west with presents for everyone including me! It must have made a great impression on me, because 68 years later I can still remember what it was—a small vial of colored sand from the desert made into a panorama of the Painted Desert. There must be something going on here because I have difficulty in remembering what I got for Christmas last year. Thinking back on it she must have had limited resources, so the gift-giving was probably something of a financial strain. The memories of a seven-year-old may be somewhat simplistic, but I also remember that she was a great favorite of the adults."

166.

And finally this:

Eighteen years ago I had a curious encounter with Frank Watson. You may remember that Frank was my parents' good friend in Berkeley from 1939 until December of 1941. He was studying zoology at UC Berkeley, same as my dad, and, along with Bob Storer, Frank helped start their independent mouse lab which lasted for about a year. High-strung and obnoxiously know-it-all, Frank had once nearly been punched by my old man for his high-handed arrogance. Fisticuffs were avoided, however, and for years afterward my dad and Frank remained good friends.

During a 2001 book signing for one of my novels at the Tattered Cover Bookstore in Denver, a clerk passed me a note from Frank Watson, who was then eighty-five and residing in north Denver. He had not seen me since I was about fifteen months old, autumn of 1941, when he, my dad, and Bob Storer were still operating their mouse lab and driving around California and Nevada keeping tabs on the birds.

Frank's Tattered Cover note asked me to phone him, which I did from my Denver hotel room. We had a long chat and subsequently exchanged several letters. Frank reminisced with me about Dad and Monique, whom he considered his best friends in Berkeley before Pearl Harbor. Then he had married, and the war drove all of us apart to distant places.

After our Denver phone call, Frank Watson and I never managed to meet face-to-face. And in 2009, at age ninety-three, Frank died. Shortly thereafter, his second wife, also named Jean, sent me a packet of letters Frank had exchanged over the years with my father. That was a beautiful gesture from Jean to me. She is one of the many persons who contributed greatly to this book and I thank her dearly. Among the documents that Jean sent to me were some recollections of Monique that Frank had scribbled on a yellow sheet of legal paper shortly before his own death.

MONIQUE

If she were there, everything would be alright.
She didn't "do" anything to make it that way, it just was.
To say I loved her is an understatement.
To say I worshipped her misses the target.
I'll say a few things, then try again.

First, there was nothing about me, or anyone else she knew, she didn't understand.

She understood her husband.

She was totally unselfish, there was nothing she needed or wanted that she didn't already have.

She never in the slightest or in any way "put on airs."

We could talk quite freely about things about which we disagreed, without rancor.

Very early in our acquaintance, Monique told me that she had had rheumatic fever. It explained why she could not always do the hikes we did.

EPILOGUE

Monique in Leysin, Switzerland, 1930.

Danny Davison contributed some real gems to my reconstruction of Monique, and for those gems, and for his friendship and humorous and instructive history of Peacock Point, I am grateful.

Late in his life when I began to hound him, Pop opened up to me as best he could, allowing a few old wounds to resurface as he passed on to me some of Monique's letters, books by my noted great-grandfather Anatole Le Braz, photographs of my mom, and his often moving, sometimes tragic, personal recollections. Prior to that he had almost never spoken to me of Monique, and I had avoided approaching him about her. Given his feelings of guilt, and his intense desire for privacy, I owe Dad for the courage it took him to share with me aspects of his relationship with Monique, and his vague memories of her final days.

During my early twenties, when I visited her in Barcelona, Mamita desired so much to resurrect my French blood, its language, culture, history, and, sadly, her own upper-crust attitudes. I wanted no part of her bourgeois social pretensions. Nevertheless, upon graduating college I wrote the early drafts of my first published novel, *The Sterile Cuckoo,* at her Barcelona apartment between June 1962 and May 1963; I thank her to this day for offering me that time and space. And even as I strained to reject Mamita's domineering personality, she forged in me the French language and my love of Spanish culture in Spain, which lay at the heart of Monique's being even if Mamita and I never discussed Monique, something that should baffle me although in my heart I understand. I suspect that Mamita gifted to me a lot of my mother's soul that I did not give her credit for. And during the 1970s she often sent me money when I was dead broke, a generosity that helped to keep my modest writing career alive through hard times.

My Uncle Nito was a friend from a distance; he sustained our family connection with occasional, yet in-depth and instructive letters from his home in Alicante, Spain. He kept me apprised of European family adventures, and, during my childhood he sent me wonderful butterflies that I softened, pinned out, and added to my Riker mounts. And when my children Luke and Tania were young and fascinated by bugs, Nito mailed them, too, many exquisite butterflies.

I never queried Nito about Monique, and he never volunteered any information about her. Go figure. Both of us were very shy.

After Mamita died in 1977, Nito asked me for a copy

of my birth certificate because I was entitled to some of her Spanish and American assets. I appealed to Pop for the document, but he didn't have a copy. So I wrote California and they sent it to me . . . the *phony* one listing Brownie as birth mother, issued when she adopted me in 1944. Which did nothing to prove that Monique had been my mother or Mamita my legitimate grandmother.

I made another request to California explaining I needed my *real* certificate, the sealed one listing Monique as my birth parent. Sacramento demanded I send them a court order to open that document. I complied, and their Bureau of Vital Statistics granted me one copy of my original birth certificate listing Monique as my mom.

I was almost forty and had never seen my true credentials. I stared at that piece of photostat paper as if I were staring at my mother herself. It included information not found on the phony certificate. For example, a complication of Monique's pregnancy was "rheumatic heart disease," the first I'd heard of that. And under the question—*Was there an operation for delivery*—the answer given was "Yes—low forceps at full dilation—episiotomy." Those facts are not replicated on the "official" document listing Brownie as my birth mother.

I put my real birth certificate in an envelope addressed to Nito and did not see that piece of paper again until I was nearly seventy-three. Nito had Mamita buried in the small town of Alella overlooking the sea near Barcelona. Her grave is beside that of Monique's sister, Ninon, who died of tuberculosis on her thirtieth birthday in 1946. I made a pilgrimage to their gravesite during the autumn of 1987.

Nito's youngest daughter, my first cousin Véronique Robert, has given me more of my mother than you could possibly imagine. I was twenty-seven when Véronique was born. And I don't believe we met in person until 1996 when she was twenty-nine and I had reached fifty-five. That's the year I traveled alongside my third wife from Sevilla, Spain, to Alicante, and we spent hours in the Robert basement with Véronique going through cardboard boxes of memorabilia—photos, childhood letters, Monique's diaries in French—discovering many treasures that I brought back to America. Later, Véronique sent me packages with more photographs of my mom and letters from her childhood days, and some trenchant information about my all but invisible grandfather, Marius Robert.

One day a special package from Spain mailed by Véronique arrived: it contained the last four letters Monique wrote in French to Mamita from Miami Beach in July 1942 just before she died. Those letters are among my most cherished possessions. They are so cheerful, and innocent, and completely ignorant of the illness that would kill their author a couple of weeks later.

I owe much of this book to Véronique's remarkable persistence in tracking down, and then sending to me, much intriguing information about the mother I never knew. On May 16, 1998, when our family had its sunny memorial service for Dad at the William Floyd estate, I met Denise Steinmacher, who was a ranger, and a museum technician and archivist for the Park Service at the estate. The Government had taken over the Floyd property when Grammie died at age ninety-six in December 1977. Several hours before Dad's public obsequies, my brothers Dave and Tim and I poured our father's ashes into a hole right beside Monique's tombstone. That's where he wanted to be, and we gave him his wish. Pop's fourth wife Jackie harbored no objections, nor had she any interest in attending our celebration back east.

Over a decade after Pop's memorial, when I got in touch with Denise Steinmacher again, she began to look for more clues to David and Monique in the Floyd estate's archives. What she discovered allowed me to fill many gaps in my folks' relationship. Denise sent me copies of rare photographs I'd never seen, also letters from Dad and Monique that I had no idea existed. She tracked down excerpts from old Mastic guest books.

And quite a slew of letters, from Dad to Grammie and Grandpa, elucidating his marriage with Monique I would never have seen without Denise's patient legwork in the Floyd estate archives.

Twelve years after my father died, Denise discovered Monique's letter dated September 30, 1938, trying to break their engagement. It is the most revealing and prescient thing Monique ever wrote. Those sorrowful words sound the only genuine note of despair I could find in all my mom's correspondence available to me. The letter explained exactly what would happen if she married my dad. And it all came to pass.

As much as my cousin Véronique, Denise has helped me to create this portrait of Monique and David's brief story. Over the many years that Denise and I have written letters back and forth and talked on the telephone, her warmth, humor, and professional expertise and interest in this project have made her one of my best friends.

Other pals who gave me information or read various drafts of the book and helped me immensely with their critiques are Maureen McCoy, Jane Ervin, Morris Witten, Jim Levy, Rick Smith, Jean Watson, Lolo Bouchage, Duck Pond, Lilah Clay, Bill Rusin, Linda Mégerlin, Ken Kahn, Susan Lang, Terra Stone, and Phaedra Greenwood. Kay Matthews I owe particularly for her willingness to read, critique, design, and format this book so that it could actually see the light of day. I am forever grateful to all for their generosity and honesty, their help, their patience, and their very valuable insights without which I would have been lost.

My younger brother, David Gelston Nichols Jr., died on February 2, 2013. He was sixty-five. Vacationing with his family in Hawaii, he went for a swim, got caught in a rip tide, and drowned. That was a blow that leaves empty a significant part of my life. I traveled back east with my first wife, Ruby, to Dave's memorial service in Mt. Kisco, New York. Ruby was the angel who got our tickets and boarding passes and guided me through the airports and onto trains and into New York City. The day before the memorial, Ruby and I visited the American Museum of Natural History in Manhattan, where, thanks to the efforts of my biologist friend, Ernest Williams, we were taken to see some of the small mammal collections contributed to the museum by my father between 1932 and 1939. A scientific assistant in the Mammalogy Department, Aja Marcato, guided us back into the collection area, and, having done a lot of research beforehand, she opened many different drawers that contained Dad's specimens of mice, bats, shrews, voles, and lemmings that he'd prepared in Florida, Nevada, and Alaska. I had never seen them before, and it was exciting to inspect his writing and the dates on each identification tag, and also to view closeup all the corked "test tubes" into which my father had placed the specimens' tiny immaculate skulls. I was thrilled when Aja encouraged me to hold a couple of stuffed lemmings that Pop had mailed to the museum from Alaska just weeks before he met Monique. And I do know that Monique had inspected most of these species with Dad during their courtship days in the late fall of 1937 and early spring of 1938.

Bless her, Aja Marcato also led us to the museum's research library and allowed us to leaf through the bound original copies of Dad's wildlife journals and field zoology notebooks connected to his expeditions for the museum. To see these original documents, which included exquisite drawings of the skins of each mammal specimen, touched me deeply. It was also powerful to keep in mind that Monique had copied out by hand many of these journals so that my father could have the records at his fingertips in Berkeley. My mom performed this travail long before there were Xerox machines.

Ruby and I took photographs of the specimen drawers and our time with Aja. I treasure the fact that, at age seventy-two, I was finally able to see the animals that my father had contributed to wildlife research long ago. Those animals had driven his love of the natural world all his born days, a love that had brought him to the American Museum and hence directly into the arms of Monique Annette Andrée Robert, the young French woman who gave me life.

———————————

CPSIA information can be obtained
at www.ICGtesting.com
Printed in the USA
LVHW011104010920
664633LV00003B/297

9 780940 875128